OFFICE OF THE UNITED NATIONS
HIGH COMMISSIONER FOR HUMAN RIGHTS
Geneva

PROFESSIONAL TRAINING SERIES No. 8/Rev.1

Istanbul Protocol

Manual on the Effective Investigation and
Documentation of Torture and Other Cruel,
Inhuman or Degrading Treatment or Punishment

UNITED NATIONS
New York and Geneva, 2004

NOTE

The designations employed and the presentation of the material in this publication do not imply the expression of any opinion whatsoever on the part of the Secretariat of the United Nations concerning the legal status of any country, territory, city or area, or of its authorities, or concerning the delimitation of its frontiers or boundaries.

*

*   *

Material contained in this publication may be freely quoted or reprinted, provided credit is given and a copy of the publication containing the reprinted material is sent to the Office of the High Commissioner for Human Rights, United Nations, 1211 Geneva 10, Switzerland.

HR/P/PT/8/Rev.1

UNITED NATIONS PUBLICATION
Sales No. E.04.XIV.3 ISBN 92-1-154156-5
ISSN 1020-1688

Manual on the Effective Investigation and Documentation of Torture and Other Cruel, Inhuman or Degrading Treatment or Punishment

Istanbul Protocol

Submitted to the
United Nations High Commissioner for Human Rights

9 August 1999

PARTICIPATING ORGANIZATIONS

Action for Torture Survivors (HRFT), Geneva
Amnesty International, London
Association for the Prevention of Torture, Geneva
Behandlungszentrum für Folteropfer, Berlin
British Medical Association (BMA), London
Center for Research and Application of Philosophy and Human Rights, Hacettepe University, Ankara
Center for the Study of Society and Medicine, Columbia University, New York
Centre Georges Devereux, University of Paris VIII, Paris
Committee against Torture, Geneva
Danish Medical Association, Copenhagen
Department of Forensic Medicine and Toxicology, University of Colombo, Colombo
Ethics Department, Dokuz Eylül Medical Faculty, Izmir, Turkey
Gaza Community Mental Health Programme, Gaza
German Medical Association, Berlin
Human Rights Foundation of Turkey (HRFT), Ankara
Human Rights Watch, New York
Indian Medical Association and the IRCT, New Delhi
Indochinese Psychiatric Clinic, Boston, United States of America
Institute for Global Studies, University of Minnesota, Minneapolis, Unites States
Instituto Latinoamericano de Salud Mental, Santiago
International Committee of the Red Cross, Geneva
International Federation of Health and Human Rights Organizations, Amsterdam, The Netherlands
International Rehabilitation Council for Torture Victims (IRCT), Copenhagen
Johannes Wier Foundation, Amsterdam, The Netherlands
Lawyers Committee for Human Rights, New York
Physicians for Human Rights Israel, Tel Aviv
Physicians for Human Rights Palestine, Gaza
Physicians for Human Rights USA, Boston
Program for the Prevention of Torture, Inter-American Institute of Human Rights,
San José
Society of Forensic Medicine Specialists, Istanbul, Turkey
Special Rapporteur on Torture, Geneva
Survivors International, San Francisco, United States
The Center for Victims of Torture (CVT), Minneapolis, United States
The Medical Foundation for the Care of Victims of Torture, London
The Trauma Centre for Survivors of Violence and Torture, Cape Town, South Africa
Turkish Medical Association, Ankara
World Medical Association, Ferney-Voltaire, France

CONTENTS

ANNEXES

CONTRIBUTING AUTHORS AND OTHER PARTICIPANTS

Project coordinators

Dr. Vincent Iacopino, Physicians for Human Rights USA, Boston, United States
Dr. Önder Özkalipçi, Human Rights Foundation of Turkey, Istanbul, Turkey
Ms. Caroline Schlar, Action for Torture Survivors (HRFT), Geneva

Editorial committee

Dr. Kathleen Allden, Indochinese Psychiatric Clinic, Boston, and Department of Psychiatry, Dartmouth Medical School, Lebanon, New Hampshire, United States
Dr. Türkcan Baykal, Human Rights Foundation of Turkey, Izmir, Turkey
Dr. Vincent Iacopino, Physicians for Human Rights USA, Boston, United States
Dr. Robert Kirschner, Physicians for Human Rights USA, Chicago, United States
Dr. Önder Özkalipçi, Human Rights Foundation of Turkey, Istanbul, Turkey
Dr. Michael Peel, The Medical Foundation for the Care of Victims of Torture, London
Dr. Hernan Reyes, Center for the Study of Society and Medicine, Columbia University, New York
Mr. James Welsh, Amnesty International, London

Rapporteurs

Dr. Kathleen Allden, Indochinese Psychiatric Clinic, Boston, and Department of Psychiatry, Dartmouth Medical School, Lebanon, New Hampshire, United States
Ms. Barbara Frey, Institute for Global Studies, University of Minnesota, Minneapolis, United States
Dr. Robert Kirschner, Physicians for Human Rights USA, Chicago, United States
Dr. Şebnem Korur Fincanci, Society of Forensic Medicine Specialists, Istanbul, Turkey
Dr. Hernan Reyes, Center for the Study of Society and Medicine, Columbia University, New York
Ms. Ann Sommerville, British Medical Association, London
Dr. Numfondo Walaza, The Trauma Centre for Survivors of Violence and Torture, Cape Town, South Africa

Contributing authors

Dr. Suat Alptekin, Forensic Medicine Department, Istanbul, Turkey
Dr. Zuhal Amato, Ethics Department, Doküz Eylul Medical Faculty, Izmir, Turkey
Dr. Alp Ayan, Human Rights Foundation of Turkey, Izmir, Turkey
Dr. Semih Aytaçlar, Sonomed, Istanbul, Turkey
Dr. Metin Bakkalci, Human Rights Foundation of Turkey, Ankara,
Dr. Ümit Biçer, Society of Forensic Medicine Specialists, Istanbul, Turkey
Dr. Yeşim Can, Human Rights Foundation of Turkey, Istanbul, Turkey
Dr. John Chisholm, British Medical Association, London
Dr. Lis Danielsen, International Rehabilitation Council for Torture Victims, Copenhagen
Dr. Hanan Diab, Physicians for Human Rights Palestine, Gaza

Mr. Jean-Michel Diez, Association for the Prevention of Torture, Geneva

Dr. Yusuf Doğar, Human Rights Foundation of Turkey, Istanbul, Turkey

Dr. Morten Ekstrom, International Rehabilitation Council for Torture Victims, Copenhagen

Professor Ravindra Fernando, Department of Forensic Medicine and Toxicology, University of Colombo, Colombo

Dr. John Fitzpatrick, Cook County Hospital, Chicago, United States

Ms. Camile Giffard, University of Essex, United Kingdom

Dr. Jill Glick, University of Chicago Children's Hospital, Chicago, United States

Dr. Emel Gökmen, Department of Neurology, Istanbul University, Istanbul, Turkey

Dr. Norbert Gurris, Behandlungszentrum für Folteropfer, Berlin

Dr. Hakan Gürvit, Department of Neurology, Istanbul University, Istanbul, Turkey

Dr. Karin Helweg-Larsen, Danish Medical Association, Copenhagen

Dr. Gill Hinshelwood, The Medical Foundation for the Care of Victims of Torture, London

Dr. Uwe Jacobs, Survivors International, San Francisco, United States

Dr. Jim Jaranson, The Center for Victims of Torture, Minneapolis, United States

Ms. Cecilia Jimenez, Association for the Prevention of Torture, Geneva

Ms. Karen Johansen Meeker, University of Minnesota Law School, Minneapolis, United States

Dr. Emre Kapkin, Human Rights Foundation of Turkey, Izmir, Turkey

Dr. Cem Kaptanoğlu, Department of Psychiatry, Osmangazi University Medical Faculty, Eskişehir, Turkey

Professor Ioanna Kuçuradi, Center for Research and Application of Philosophy and Human Rights, Hacettepe University, Ankara

Mr. Basem Lafi, Gaza Community Mental Health Programme, Gaza

Dr. Elizabeth Lira, Instituto Latinoamericano de Salud Mental, Santiago

Dr. Veli Lök, Human Rights Foundation of Turkey, Izmir, Turkey

Dr. Michèle Lorand, Cook County Hospital, Chicago, United States

Dr. Ruchama Marton, Physicians for Human Rights-Israel, Tel Aviv

Ms. Elisa Massimino, Lawyers Committee for Human Rights, New York

Ms. Carol Mottet, Legal Consultant, Bern

Dr. Fikri Öztop, Department of Pathology, Ege University Medical Faculty, Izmir, Turkey

Mr. Alan Parra, Office of the Special Rapporteur on Torture, Geneva

Dr. Beatrice Patsalides, Survivors International, San Francisco, United States

Dr. Jean Pierre Restellini, Human Rights Awareness Unit, Directorate of Human Rights, Council of Europe, Strasbourg, France

Mr. Nigel Rodley, Special Rapporteur on Torture, Geneva

Dr. Füsun Sayek, Turkish Medical Association, Ankara

Dr. Françoise Sironi, Centre Georges Devereux, University of Paris VIII, Paris

Dr. Bent Sorensen, International Rehabilitation Council for Torture Victims, Copenhagen and Committee against Torture, Geneva

Dr. Nezir Suyugül, Forensic Medicine Department, Istanbul, Turkey

Ms. Asmah Tareen, University of Minnesota Law School, Minneapolis, United States

Dr. Henrik Klem Thomsen, Department of Pathology, Bispebjerg Hospital, Copenhagen

Dr. Morris Tidball-Binz, Program for the Prevention of Torture, Inter-American Institute of Human Rights, San José

Dr. Nuray Türksoy, Human Rights Foundation of Turkey, Istanbul, Turkey

Ms. Hülya Üçpinar, Human Rights Office, Izmir Bar Association, Izmir, Turkey

Dr. Adriaan van Es, Johannes Wier Foundation, Amsterdam, The Netherlands

Mr. Ralf Wiedemann, University of Minnesota Law School, Minneapolis, United States

Dr. Mark Williams, The Center for Victims of Torture, Minneapolis, United States

Participants

Mr. Alessio Bruni, Committee against Torture, Geneva

Dr. Eyad El Sarraj, Gaza Community Mental Health Programme, Gaza

Dr. Rosa Garcia-Peltoniemi, The Center for Victims of Torture, Minneapolis, United States

Dr. Ole Hartling, Danish Medical Association, Copenhagen

Dr. Hans Petter Hougen, Danish Medical Association, Copenhagen

Dr. Delon Human, World Medical Association, Ferney-Voltaire, France

Dr. Dario Lagos, Equipo Argentino de Trabajo e Investigación Psicosocial, Buenos Aires

Dr. Frank Ulrich Montgomery, German Medical Association, Berlin

Mr. Daniel Prémont, United Nations Voluntary Fund for Victims of Torture, Geneva

Dr. Jagdish C. Sobti, Indian Medical Association, New Delhi

Mr. Trevor Stevens, European Committee for the Prevention of Torture, Strasbourg, France

Mr. Turgut Tarhanli, International Relations and Human Rights Department, Boğazici University, Istanbul, Turkey

Mr. Wilder Taylor, Human Rights Watch, New York

Dr. Joergen Thomsen, International Rehabilitation Council for Torture Victims, Copenhagen

This project was funded with the generous support of the United Nations Voluntary Fund for Victims of Torture; the Division for Human Rights and Humanitarian Policy of the Federal Department of Foreign Affairs, Switzerland; the Office for Democratic Institutions and Human Rights of the Organization for Security and Cooperation in Europe; the Swedish Red Cross, the Human Rights Foundation of Turkey and Physicians for Human Rights. Additional support was contributed by the Center for Victims of Torture; the Turkish Medical Association; the International Rehabilitation Council for Torture Victims; Amnesty International Switzerland and the Christian Association for the Abolition of Torture Switzerland.

The printing of the revised version of the manual was funded with the financial support of the European Commission. The work of art displayed on the cover page of the revised version was donated to the United Nations Voluntary Fund for Victims of Torture by the Centre for Victims of Torture (CVICT), Nepal.

INTRODUCTION

Torture is defined in this manual in the words of the United Nations Convention against Torture and Other Cruel, Inhuman or Degrading Treatment or Punishment, 1984:

[T]orture means any act by which severe pain or suffering, whether physical or mental, is intentionally inflicted on a person for such purposes as obtaining from him or a third person information or a confession, punishing him for an act he or a third person, has committed or is suspected of having committed, or intimidating or coercing him or a third person, or for any reason based on discrimination of any kind, when such pain or suffering is inflicted by or at the instigation of or with the consent or acquiescence of a public official or other person acting in an official capacity. It does not include pain or suffering arising only from, inherent in or incidental to lawful sanctions.[1]

Torture is a profound concern of the world community. Its purpose is to destroy deliberately not only the physical and emotional well-being of individuals but also, in some instances, the dignity and will of entire communities. It concerns all members of the human family because it impugns the very meaning of our existence and our hopes for a brighter future.[2]

Although international human rights and humanitarian law consistently prohibit torture under any circumstance (see chapter I), torture and ill-treatment are practised in more than half of the world's countries.[3, 4] The striking disparity between the absolute prohibition of torture and its prevalence in the world today demonstrates the need for States to identify and implement effective measures to protect individuals from torture and ill-treatment. This manual was developed to enable States to address one of the most fundamental concerns in protecting individuals from torture—effective documentation. Such documentation brings evidence of torture and ill-treatment to light so that perpetrators may be held accountable for their actions and the interests of justice may be served. The documentation methods contained in this manual are also applicable to other contexts, including human rights investigations and monitoring, political asylum evaluations, the defence of individuals who "confess" to crimes during torture and needs assessments for the care of torture victims, among others. In the case of health professionals who are coerced into neglect, misrepresentation or falsification of evidence of torture, this manual also provides an international point of reference for health professionals and adjudicators alike.

During the past two decades, much has been learned about torture and its consequences, but no international guidelines for documentation were available prior to the development of this manual. The *Istanbul Protocol: Manual on the Effective Investigation and Documentation of Torture and Other Cruel, Inhuman or Degrading Treatment or Punishment* is intended to serve as international guidelines for the assessment of persons who allege torture and ill-treatment, for investigating cases of alleged torture and for reporting findings to the judiciary or any other investigative body. This manual includes principles for the effective investigation and documentation of torture,

---

[1] Since 1982, the recommendations concerning United Nations assistance to victims of torture made by the Board of Trustees of the United Nations Voluntary Fund for Victims of Torture to the Secretary-General of the United Nations, are based on article 1 of the Declaration on the Protection of All Persons from Being Subjected to Torture and Other Cruel, Inhuman or Degrading Treatment or Punishment, which provides that "Torture constitutes an aggravated and deliberate form of cruel, inhuman or degrading treatment or punishment" and that "It does not include pain or suffering arising only from, inherent in or incidental to, lawful sanctions to the extent consistent with the Standard Minimum Rules for the Treatment of Prisoners", as well as on all other relevant international instruments.

[2] V. Iacopino, "Treatment of survivors of political torture: commentary", *The Journal of Ambulatory Care Management*, vol. 21 (2) (1998), pp. 5-13.

[3] Amnesty International, *Amnesty International Report 1999* (London, AIP, 1999).

[4] M. Başoglu, "Prevention of torture and care of survivors: an integrated approach", *The Journal of the American Medical Association (JAMA)*, vol. 270 (1993), pp. 606-611.

and other cruel, inhuman or degrading treatment or punishment (see annex I). These principles outline minimum standards for States in order to ensure the effective documentation of torture.[5] The guidelines contained in this manual are not presented as a fixed protocol. Rather, they represent minimum standards based on the principles and should be used taking into account available resources. The manual and principles are the result of three years of analysis, research and drafting, undertaken by more than 75 experts in law, health and human rights, representing 40 organizations or institutions from 15 countries. The conceptualization and preparation of this manual was a collaborative effort between forensic scientists, physicians, psychologists, human-rights monitors and lawyers working in Chile, Costa Rica, Denmark, France, Germany, India, Israel, the Netherlands, South Africa, Sri Lanka, Switzerland, Turkey, the United Kingdom, the United States of America, and the occupied Palestinian territories.

---

[5] The Principles on the Effective Investigation and Documentation of Torture and Other Cruel, Inhuman or Degrading Treatment or Punishment are annexed to General Assembly resolution 55/89 of 4 December 2000 and to Commission on Human Rights resolution 2000/43 of 20 April 2000, both adopted without a vote.

CHAPTER I

RELEVANT INTERNATIONAL LEGAL STANDARDS

1.   The right to be free from torture is firmly established under international law. The Universal Declaration of Human Rights, the International Covenant on Civil and Political Rights and the Convention against Torture and Other Cruel, Inhuman or Degrading Treatment or Punishment all expressly prohibit torture. Similarly, several regional instruments establish the right to be free from torture. The American Convention on Human Rights, the African Charter on Human and Peoples' Rights and the European Convention for the Protection of Human Rights and Fundamental Freedoms all contain express prohibitions of torture.

A.   International humanitarian law

2.   The international treaties governing armed conflicts establish international humanitarian law or the law of war. The prohibition of torture under international humanitarian law is only a small, but important, part of the wider protection these treaties provide for all victims of war. The four Geneva Conventions of 1949 have been ratified by 188 States. They establish rules for the conduct of international armed conflict and, especially, for the treatment of persons who do not, or who no longer, take part in hostilities, including the wounded, the captured and civilians. All four conventions prohibit the infliction of torture and other forms of ill-treatment. Two Protocols of 1977, additional to the Geneva Conventions, expand the protection and scope of these conventions. Protocol I (ratified to date by 153 States) covers international conflicts. Protocol II (ratified to date by 145 States) covers non-international conflicts.

3.   More important to the purpose here, however, is what is known as "Common Article 3", found in all four conventions. Common Article 3 applies to armed conflicts "not of an international character", no further definition being given. It is taken to define core obligations that must be respected in all armed conflicts and not just in international wars between countries. This is generally taken to mean that no matter what the nature of a war or conflict, certain basic rules cannot be abrogated. The prohibition of torture is one of these and represents an element common to international humanitarian law and human rights law.

4.   Common Article 3 states:

… the following acts are and shall remain prohibited at any time and in any place whatsoever… violence to life and person, in particular murder of all kinds, mutilation, cruel treatment and torture; … outrages upon personal dignity, in particular humiliating and degrading treatment…

5.   As the Special Rapporteur on the question of torture, Nigel Rodley, has stated:

The prohibition of torture or other ill-treatment could hardly be formulated in more absolute terms. In the words of the official commentary on the text by the International Committee of the Red Cross (ICRC), no possible loophole is left; there can be no excuse, no attenuating circumstances.[6]

6.   A further link between international humanitarian law and human rights law is found in the preamble to Protocol II, which itself regulates non-international armed conflicts (such as fully-fledged civil wars), and which states that: "… international instruments relating to human rights offer a basic protection to the human person."[7]

B.   The United Nations

7.   The United Nations has sought for many years to develop universally applicable standards to ensure adequate protection for all persons against torture or cruel, inhuman or degrading treatment. The conventions, declarations and resolutions adopted by the Member States of the United Nations clearly state that there may be no exception to the prohibition of torture and establish other obligations to ensure protection against such abuses. Among the most important of these instruments are the Universal Declaration of Human Rights,[8] the International Covenant on Civil and Political Rights,[9] the Standard Minimum Rules for the Treatment of Prisoners,[10] the Declaration on the Protection of All Persons from Being Subjected to Torture and Other Cruel, Inhuman or Degrading Treatment or Punishment (Declaration on the Protection against Torture),[11] the Code of Conduct on

---

[6] N. Rodley, *The Treatment of Prisoners under International Law*, 2nd ed. (Oxford, Clarendon Press, 1999), p. 58.

[7] Second preambular paragraph of Protocol II (1977), additional to the Geneva Conventions of 1949.

[8] General Assembly resolution 217 A (III) of 10 December 1948, art. 5; see *Official Records of the General Assembly, Third Session* (A/810), p. 71.

[9] Entered into force on 23 March 1976; see General Assembly resolution 2200 A (XXI), of 16 December 1966, annex, art. 7; *Official Records of the General Assembly, Twenty-first Session, Supplement No. 16* (A/6316), p. 52, and United Nations, *Treaty Series*, vol. 999, p.171.

[10] Adopted on 30 August 1955 by the First United Nations Congress on the Prevention of Crime and the Treatment of Offenders.

[11] General Assembly resolution 3452 (XXX) of 9 December 1975, annex, arts. 2 and 4; see *Official Records of the General Assembly, Thirtieth Session, Supplement No. 34* (A/10034), p. 91.

Law Enforcement,[12] the Principles of Medical Ethics Relevant to the Role of Health Personnel Particularly Physicians, in the Protection of Prisoners and Detainees against Torture and Other Cruel, Inhuman or Degrading Treatment or Punishment (Principles of Medical Ethics),[13] the Convention against Torture and Other Cruel, Inhuman or Degrading Treatment or Punishment (Convention against Torture),[14] the Body of Principles for the Protection of all Persons under Any Form of Detention or Imprisonment (Body of Principles on Detention)[15] and the Basic Principles for the Treatment of Prisoners.[16]

8. The United Nations Convention against Torture does not cover pain or suffering arising only from, inherent in or incidental to lawful sanctions.[17]

9. Other United Nations human rights bodies and mechanisms have taken action to develop standards for the prevention of torture and standards involving the obligation of States to investigate allegations of torture. These bodies and mechanisms include the Committee against Torture, the Human Rights Committee, the Commission on Human Rights, the Special Rapporteur on the question of torture, the Special Rapporteur on violence against women and country-specific special rapporteurs appointed by the Commission on Human Rights.

1. *Legal obligations to prevent torture*

10. The international instruments cited above establish certain obligations that States must respect to ensure protection against torture. These include:

(*a*) Taking effective legislative, administrative, judicial or other measures to prevent acts of torture. No exceptions, including war, may be invoked as justification for torture (art. 2 of the Convention against Torture and

art. 3 of the Declaration on the Protection against Torture);

(*b*) Not expelling, returning (*refouler*) or extraditing a person to a country when there are substantial grounds for believing he or she would be tortured (art. 3 of the Convention against Torture);

(*c*) Criminalization of acts of torture, including complicity or participation therein (art. 4 of the Convention against Torture, principle 7 of the Body of Principles on Detention, art. 7 of the Declaration on the Protection against Torture and paras. 31-33 of the Standard Minimum Rules for the Treatment of Prisoners);

(*d*) Undertaking to make torture an extraditable offence and assisting other States parties in connection with criminal proceedings brought in respect of torture (arts. 8 and 9 of the Convention against Torture);

(*e*) Limiting the use of incommunicado detention; ensuring that detainees are held in places officially recognized as places of detention; ensuring the names of persons responsible for their detention are kept in registers readily available and accessible to those concerned, including relatives and friends; recording the time and place of all interrogations, together with the names of those present; and granting physicians, lawyers and family members access to detainees (art. 11 of the Convention against Torture; principles 11-13, 15-19 and 23 of the Body of Principles on Detention; paras. 7, 22 and 37 of the Standard Minimum Rules for the Treatment of Prisoners);

(*f*) Ensuring that education and information regarding the prohibition of torture is included in the training of law enforcement personnel (civil and military), medical personnel, public officials and other appropriate persons (art. 10 of the Convention against Torture, art. 5 of the Declaration on the Protection against Torture, para. 54 of the Standard Minimum Rules for the Treatment of Prisoners);

(*g*) Ensuring that any statement that is established to have been made as a result of torture shall not be invoked as evidence in any proceedings, except against a person accused of torture as evidence that the statement was made (art. 15 of the Convention against Torture, art. 12 of the Declaration on the Protection against Torture);

(*h*) Ensuring that the competent authorities undertake a prompt and impartial investigation, whenever there are reasonable grounds to believe that torture has been committed (art. 12 of the Convention against Torture, principles 33 and 34 of the Body of Principles on Detention, art. 9 of the Declaration on the Protection against Torture);

(*i*) Ensuring that victims of torture have the right to redress and adequate compensation (arts. 13 and 14 of the Convention against Torture, art. 11 of the Declaration on the Protection against Torture, paras. 35 and 36 of the Standard Minimum Rules for the Treatment of Prisoners);

(*j*) Ensuring that the alleged offender or offenders is subject to criminal proceedings if an investigation establishes that an act of torture appears to have been commit-

---

[12] General Assembly resolution 34/169 of 17 December 1979, annex, art. 5; see *Official Records of the General Assembly, Thirty-fourth Session, Supplement No. 46* (A/34/46), p. 186.

[13] General Assembly resolution 37/194 of 18 December 1982, annex, principles 2–5; see *Official Records of the General Assembly, Thirty-seventh Session, Supplement No. 51* (A/37/51), p. 211.

[14] Entered into force on 26 June 1987; see General Assembly resolution 39/46 of 10 December 1984, annex, art. 2, *Official Records of the General Assembly, Thirty-ninth Session, Supplement No. 51* (A/39/51), p. 197.

[15] General Assembly resolution 43/173 of 9 December 1988, annex, principle 6; see *Official Records of the General Assembly, Forty-third Session, Supplement No. 49* (A/43/49), p. 298.

[16] General Assembly resolution 45/111 of 14 December 1990, annex, principle 1; see *Official Records of the General Assembly, Forty-fifth Session, Supplement No. 49* (A/45/49), p. 200.

[17] For an interpretation of what constitutes "lawful sanctions", see the report of the Special Rapporteur on torture to the fifty-third session of the Commission on Human Rights (E/CN.4/1997/7, paras. 3-11), in which the Special Rapporteur expressed the view that the administration of punishments such as stoning to death, flogging and amputation cannot be deemed lawful simply because the punishment has been authorized in a procedurally legitimate manner. The interpretation put forward by the Special Rapporteur, which is consistent with the positions of the Human Rights Committee and other United Nations mechanisms, was endorsed by resolution 1998/38 of the Commission on Human Rights, which "[r]eminds Governments that corporal punishment can amount to cruel, inhuman or degrading treatment or even to torture".

ted. If an allegation of other forms of cruel, inhuman or degrading treatment or punishment is considered to be well founded, the alleged offender or offenders shall be subject to criminal, disciplinary or other appropriate proceedings (art. 7 of the Convention against Torture, art. 10 of the Declaration on the Protection against Torture).

2. *United Nations bodies and mechanisms*

(a) *Committee against Torture*

11. The Committee against Torture monitors implementation of the Convention against Torture and Other Cruel, Inhuman or Degrading Treatment or Punishment. The Committee consists of 10 experts appointed because of their "high moral standing and recognized competence in the field of human rights". Under article 19 of the Convention against Torture, the States parties submit to the Committee, through the Secretary-General, reports on the measures they have taken to give effect to their undertakings under the Convention. The Committee examines how the provisions of the Convention have been incorporated into domestic law and monitors how this functions in practice. Each report is considered by the Committee, which may make general comments and recommendations and include this information in its annual report to the States parties and to the General Assembly. These procedures take place in public meetings.

12. Under article 20 of the Convention against Torture, if the Committee receives reliable information that appears to contain well-founded indications that torture is being systematically practised in the territory of a State party, the Committee must invite that State party to cooperate in the examination of the information and, to this end, to submit observations with regard to the information concerned. The Committee may, if it decides that this is warranted, designate one or more of its members to make a confidential inquiry and to report to the Committee urgently. In agreement with that State party, that inquiry may include a visit to its territory. After examining the findings of its member or members, the Committee transmits these findings to the State party concerned together with any comments or suggestions that seem appropriate in view of the situation. All the proceedings of the Committee under article 20 are confidential, and, at all stages of the proceedings, the cooperation of the State party is sought. After completion of these proceedings, the Committee may, after consultations with the State party concerned, decide to include a summary account of the results of the proceedings in its annual report to the other States parties and to the General Assembly.[18]

13. Under article 22 of the Convention against Torture, a State party may at any time recognize the competence of the Committee to receive and consider individual complaints from or on behalf of individuals subject to its jurisdiction who claim to be victims of a violation by a State party of the provisions of the Convention against Torture. The Committee then considers these communications confidentially and shall forward its view to the State party concerned and to the individual. Only 39 of the 112 States parties that have ratified the Convention have also recognized the applicability of article 22.

14. Among the concerns addressed by the Committee in its annual reports to the General Assembly is the necessity of States parties to comply with articles 12 and 13 on the Convention against Torture to ensure that prompt and impartial investigations of all complaints of torture are undertaken. For example, the Committee has stated that it considers a delay of 15 months in investigating allegations of torture to be unreasonably long and not in compliance with article 12.[19] The Committee has also noted that article 13 does not require a formal submission of a complaint of torture, but that "[i]t is sufficient for torture only to have been alleged by the victim for [a State Party] to be under an obligation promptly and impartially to examine the allegation".[20]

(b) *Human Rights Committee*

15. The Human Rights Committee was established pursuant to article 28 of the International Covenant on Civil and Political Rights and the requirement to monitor implementation of the Covenant in the States parties. The Committee is composed of 18 independent experts who are expected to be persons of high moral character and of recognized competence in the field of human rights.

16. States parties to the Covenant must submit reports every five years on the measures they have adopted to give effect to the rights recognized in the Covenant and on progress made in the enjoyment of those rights. The Human Rights Committee examines the reports through a dialogue with representatives of the State party whose report is under consideration. The Committee then adopts concluding observations summarizing its main concerns and making appropriate suggestions and recommendations to the State party. The Committee also prepares general comments interpreting specific articles of the Covenant to guide States parties in their reporting, as well as their implementation of the Covenant's provisions. In one such general comment, the Committee undertook to clarify article 7 of the International Covenant on Civil and Political Rights, which states that no one shall be subject to torture or to cruel, inhuman or degrading treatment or punishment. In the general comments on article 7 of the Covenant in the report of the Committee, it specifically noted that prohibiting torture or making it a crime was not sufficient implementation of article 7.[21] The Committee stated: "... States must ensure an effective protection through some machinery of control. Complaints about ill-treatment must be investigated effectively by competent authorities."

17. On 10 April 1992, the Committee adopted new general comments on article 7, further developing the previous comments. The Committee reinforced its reading of article 7 by stating that "[c]omplaints must be investi-

---

[18] It should be pointed out, however, that application of article 20 can be limited because of a reservation by a State party, in which case article 20 is not applicable.

[19] See Communication 8/1991, para. 185, Report of the Committee against Torture to the General Assembly (A/49/44) of 12 June 1994.

[20] See Communication 6/1990, para. 10.4, Report of the Committee against Torture to the General Assembly (A/50/44) of 26 July 1995.

[21] United Nations, document A/37/40 (1982).

gated promptly and impartially by competent authorities so as to make the remedy effective". Where a State has ratified the first Optional Protocol to the International Covenant on Civil and Political Rights, an individual may submit a communication to the Committee complaining that his rights under the Covenant have been violated. If found admissible, the Committee issues a decision on the merits, which is made public in its annual report.

(c) *Commission on Human Rights*

18. The Commission on Human Rights is the primary human rights body of the United Nations. It is composed of 53 Member States elected by the Economic and Social Council for three-year terms. The Commission meets annually for six weeks in Geneva to act on human rights issues. The Commission may initiate studies and fact-finding missions, draft conventions and declarations for approval by higher United Nations bodies and discuss specific human rights violations in public or private sessions. On 6 June 1967, the Economic and Social Council, in resolution 1235, authorized the Commission to examine allegations of gross violations of human rights and to "make a thorough study of situations which reveal a consistent pattern of violations of human rights".[22] Under this mandate, the Commission has, among other procedures, adopted resolutions expressing concern about human rights violations and has appointed special rapporteurs to address human rights violations falling under a particular theme. The Commission has also adopted resolutions regarding torture and other cruel, inhuman or degrading treatment or punishment. In its resolution 1998/38, the Commission stressed that "all allegations of torture or cruel, inhuman or degrading treatment or punishment should be promptly and impartially examined by the competent national authority".

(d) *Special Rapporteur on the question of torture*

19. In 1985, the Commission decided, in resolution 1985/33, to appoint a Special Rapporteur on the question of torture. The Special Rapporteur is charged with seeking and receiving credible and reliable information on questions relevant to torture and to respond to that information without delay. The Commission has continued to renew the Special Rapporteur's mandate in subsequent resolutions.

20. The Special Rapporteur's authority to monitor extends to all Member States of the United Nations and to all States with observer status, regardless of the State's ratification of the Convention against Torture. The Special Rapporteur establishes contact with Governments, asks them for information on legislative and administrative measures taken to prevent torture, requests them to remedy any consequences and asks them to respond to information alleging the actual occurrence of torture. The Special Rapporteur also receives requests for urgent action, which he or she brings to the attention of the Governments concerned in order to ensure protection of an individual's right to physical and mental integrity. In addition, the Special Rapporteur holds consultations with gov-

ernment representatives who wish to meet with him or her and, in accordance with the position's mandate, makes *in situ* visits to some parts of the world. The Special Rapporteur submits reports to the Commission on Human Rights and to the General Assembly. These reports describe actions that the Special Rapporteur has taken under his or her mandate and persistently draw attention to the importance of prompt investigation of torture allegations. In the Report of the Special Rapporteur on the question of torture of 12 January 1995, the Special Rapporteur, Nigel Rodley, made a series of recommendations. In paragraph 926 (*g*) of the report, he stated:

When a detainee or relative or lawyer lodges a torture complaint, an inquiry should always take place… Independent national authorities, such as a national commission or ombudsman with investigatory and/ or prosecutorial powers, should be established to receive and to investigate complaints. Complaints about torture should be dealt with immediately and should be investigated by an independent authority with no relation to that which is investigating or prosecuting the case against the alleged victim.[23]

21. The Special Rapporteur emphasized this recommendation in his report of 9 January 1996.[24] Discussing his concern about torture practices, the Special Rapporteur pointed out in paragraph 136 that "both under general international law and under the Convention against Torture and Other Cruel, Inhuman or Degrading Treatment or Punishment, States are obliged to investigate allegations of torture".

(e) *Special Rapporteur on violence against women*

22. The Special Rapporteur on violence against women was established in 1994 by resolution 1994/45 of the Commission on Human Rights and that mandate was renewed by resolution 1997/44. The Special Rapporteur has established procedures to seek clarification and information from Governments, in a humanitarian spirit, on specific cases of alleged violence in order to identify and investigate specific situations and allegations of violence against women in any country. These communications may concern one or more individuals identified by name or information of a more general nature relating to a prevailing situation condoning or perpetrating violence against women. The definition of gender-based violence against women used by the Special Rapporteur is taken from the Declaration on the Elimination of Violence against Women, adopted by the General Assembly in resolution 48/104 of 20 December 1993. Urgent appeals may be sent by the Special Rapporteur in cases of gender-based violence against women that involve or may involve an imminent threat or fear of threat to the right to life or physical integrity of a person. The Special Rapporteur urges the competent national authorities not only to provide comprehensive information on the case but also to carry out an independent and impartial investigation concerning the case transmitted and to take immediate action to ensure that no further violation of the human rights of women occur.

[22] Ibid., E/4393.

[23] Ibid., E/CN.4/1995/34.
[24] Ibid., E/CN.4/1996/35.

23. The Special Rapporteur reports annually to the Commission on Human Rights on communications sent to Governments and on replies received by him or her. On the basis of information received from Governments and other reliable sources, the Special Rapporteur makes recommendations to the Governments concerned with a view to finding durable solutions to the elimination of violence against women in any country. The Special Rapporteur may send follow-up communications to Governments when no replies have been received or when insufficient information has been provided. Should a particular situation of violence against women in any given country persist and information received by the Special Rapporteur indicate that no measures are or have been taken by a Government to ensure the protection of the human rights of women, the Special Rapporteur may consider the possibility of seeking permission from the Government concerned to visit that country in order to carry out an on-site fact-finding mission.

(f) United Nations Voluntary Fund for Victims of Torture

24. The physical and psychological after-effects of torture can be devastating and last for years, affecting not only the victims but also members of their families. Assistance in recovering from the trauma suffered can be obtained from organizations that specialize in assisting victims of torture. In December 1981, the General Assembly established the United Nations Voluntary Fund for Victims of Torture to receive voluntary contributions for distribution to non-governmental organizations (NGOs) that provide psychological, medical, social, economic, legal and other forms of humanitarian assistance to victims of torture and members of their families. Depending on the voluntary contributions available, the Fund may finance about 200 NGO projects assisting about 80,000 victims of torture and members of their families in about 80 countries worldwide. The Fund financed the drafting and translation of the present manual and recommended its publication in the Professional Training Series of the Office of the United Nations High Commissioner for Human Rights, following a recommendation of its Board of Trustees, which subsidizes a limited number of projects to train health professionals and others on how to provide specialized assistance to victims of torture.

C. Regional organizations

25. Regional bodies have also contributed to the development of standards for the prevention of torture. These bodies include the Inter-American Commission on Human Rights, the Inter-American Court of Human Rights, the European Court of Human Rights, the European Committee for the Prevention of Torture and the African Commission on Human Rights.

1. The Inter-American Commission on Human Rights and the Inter-American Court of Human Rights

26. On 22 November 1969, the Organization of American States adopted the American Convention on Human Rights, which entered into force on 18 July 1978.[25] Article 5 of the Convention states:

1. Every person has the right to have his physical, mental, and moral integrity respected.

2. No one shall be subjected to torture or to cruel, inhuman, or degrading punishment or treatment. All persons deprived of their liberty shall be treated with respect for the inherent dignity of the human person.

27. Article 33 of the Convention provides for the establishment of the Inter-American Commission on Human Rights and the Inter-American Court of Human Rights. As stated in its regulations, the Commission's principal function is to promote the observance and defence of human rights and to serve as an advisory body to the Organization of American States in this area.[26] In fulfilling this function, the Commission has looked to the Inter-American Convention to Prevent and Punish Torture to guide its interpretation of what is meant by torture under article 5.[27] The Inter-American Convention to Prevent and Punish Torture was adopted by the Organization of American States on 9 December 1985 and entered into force on 28 February 1987.[28] Article 2 of the Convention defines torture as:

…any act intentionally performed whereby physical or mental pain or suffering is inflicted on a person for purposes of criminal investigation, as a means of intimidation, as personal punishment, as a preventive measure, as a penalty, or for any other purpose. Torture shall also be understood to be the use of methods upon a person intended to obliterate the personality of the victim or to diminish his physical or mental capacities, even if they do not cause physical pain or mental anguish.

28. Under article 1, the States parties to the Convention undertake to prevent and punish torture in accordance with the terms of the Convention. States parties to the Convention are required to conduct an immediate and proper investigation into any allegation that torture has occurred within their jurisdiction.

29. Article 8 provides that "States Parties shall guarantee that any person making an accusation of having been subjected to torture within their jurisdiction shall have the right to an impartial examination of his case". Likewise, if there is an accusation or well-grounded reason to believe that an act of torture has been committed within their jurisdiction, the States parties must guarantee that their respective authorities will proceed properly and immediately to conduct an investigation into the case and initiate, whenever appropriate, the corresponding criminal process.

30. In one of its 1998 country reports, the Commission noted that an obstacle to the effective prosecution of torturers is the lack of independence in an investigation of claims of torture, as the investigation is required to be undertaken by federal bodies likely to be acquainted with

[25] Organization of American States, *Treaty Series*, No. 36, and United Nations, *Treaty Series,* vol. 1144, p. 123, reprinted in "Basic documents pertaining to human rights in the inter-American system" (OEA/Scr. L.V/II.82, document 6, rev. 1), p. 25 (1992).

[26] "Regulations of the Inter-American Commission on Human Rights" (OEA/Ser.L.V/II.92), document 31, rev. 3 of 3 May 1996, art. (1).

[27] See case 10.832, report No. 35/96, Inter-American Commission on Human Rights Annual Report 1997, para. 75.

[28] Organization of American States, *Treaty Series,* No. 67.

parties accused of committing torture.[29] The Commission cited article 8 to underscore the importance of an "impartial examination" of each case.[30]

31. The Inter-American Court of Human Rights has addressed the necessity of investigating claims of violations of the American Convention on Human Rights. In its decision in the Velásquez Rodríguez case, judgement of 29 July 1988, the Court stated that:

The State is obligated to investigate every situation involving a violation of the rights protected by the Convention. If the State apparatus acts in such a way that the violation goes unpunished and the victim's full enjoyment of such rights is not restored as soon as possible, the State has failed to comply with its duty to ensure the free and full exercise of those rights to the persons within its jurisdiction.

32. Article 5 of the Convention provides for the right to be free from torture. Although the case dealt specifically with the issue of disappearance, one of the rights referred to by the Court as guaranteed by the American Convention on Human Rights is the right not to be subjected to torture or other forms of ill-treatment.

2. The European Court of Human Rights

33. On 4 November 1950, the Council of Europe adopted the European Convention for the Protection of Human Rights and Fundamental Freedoms, which entered into force on 3 September 1953.[31] Article 3 of the European Convention states that "No one shall be subjected to torture or to inhuman or degrading treatment or punishment". The European Convention established control mechanisms consisting of the European Court and the European Commission of Human Rights. Since the reform that entered into force on 1 November 1998, a new permanent Court has replaced the former Court and Commission. The right of individual applications is now mandatory, and all victims have direct access to the Court. The Court has had the occasion to consider the necessity of investigating allegations of torture as a way of ensuring the rights guaranteed by article 3.

34. The first judgement on this issue was the decision in the Aksoy v. Turkey case (100/1995/606/694), delivered on 18 December 1996.[32] In that case, the Court considered that:

[w]here an individual is taken into police custody in good health but is found to be injured at the time of release, it is incumbent on the State to provide a plausible explanation as to the causing of the injury, failing which a clear issue arises under Article 3 of the Convention.[33]

35. The Court went on to hold that the injuries inflicted on the applicant resulted from torture and that article 3 had been violated.[34] Furthermore, the Court interpreted article 13 of the Convention, which provides for the right to an effective remedy before a national authority, as imposing an obligation to investigate claims of torture thoroughly. Considering the "fundamental importance of the prohibition of torture" and the vulnerability of torture victims, the Court held that "Article 13 imposes, without prejudice to any other remedy available under the domestic system, an obligation on States to carry out a thorough and effective investigation of incidents of torture".[35]

36. According to the Court's interpretation, the notion of an "effective remedy" in article 13 entails a thorough investigation of every "arguable claim" of torture. The Court noted that although the Convention has no express provision, such as article 12 of the Convention against Torture and Other Cruel, Inhuman or Degrading Treatment or Punishment, "such a requirement is implicit in the notion of an 'effective remedy' under Article 13".[36] The Court then found that the State had violated article 13 by failing to investigate the applicant's allegation of torture.[37]

37. In a judgement of 28 October 1998 in the case of Assenov and Others v. Bulgaria (90/1997/874/1086), the Court went even further in recognizing an obligation for the State to investigate allegations of torture not only under article 13 but also under article 3. In this case, a young Romany arrested by the police showed medical evidence of beatings, but it was impossible to assess, on the basis of available evidence, whether these injuries were caused by his father or by the police. The Court recognized that "the degree of bruising found by the doctor who examined Mr. Assenov ...indicates that the latter's injuries, whether caused by his father or by the police, were sufficiently serious to amount to ill-treatment within the scope of Article 3".[38] Contrary to the Commission that held that there was no violation of article 3, the Court did not stop there. It went on and considered that the facts raised "a reasonable suspicion that these injuries may have been caused by the police".[39] Hence the Court held that:

[I]n these circumstances, where an individual raises an arguable claim that he has been seriously ill-treated by the police or other such agents of the State unlawfully and in breach of Article 3, that provision, read in conjunction with the State's general duty under Article 1 of the Convention "to secure to everyone within their jurisdiction the rights and freedoms defined in [the] Convention", requires by implication that there should be an effective official investigation. This investigation... should be capable of leading to the identification and punishment of those responsible. If this were not the case, the general legal prohibition of torture and inhuman and degrading treatment and punishment, despite its fundamental importance..., would be ineffective in practice and it would be possible in some cases for agents of the State to abuse the rights of those within their control with virtual impunity.[40]

38. For the first time, the Court concluded that a violation of article 3 had occurred, not from ill-treatment per se but from a failure to carry out effective official investigation on the allegation of ill-treatment. In addi-

---

[29] Inter-American Commission on Human Rights, Report on the Situation of Human Rights in Mexico, 1998, para. 323.

[30] Ibid., para. 324.

[31] United Nations, Treaty Series, vol. 213, p. 222.

[32] See Additional Protocols Nos. 3, 5 and 8, which entered into force on 21 September 1970, 20 December 1971 and 1 January 1990, European Treaty Series Nos. 45, 46 and 118, respectively.

[33] See European Court of Human Rights, Reports of Judgments and Decisions 1996–VI, para. 61.

[34] Ibid., para. 64.

[35] Ibid., para. 98.

[36] Ibid.

[37] Ibid., para. 100.

[38] Ibid., Reports of Judgments and Decisions 1998–VIII, para. 95.

[39] Ibid., para. 101.

[40] Ibid., para. 102.

tion, the Court reiterated its position in the Aksoy case and concluded that there had also been a violation of article 13. The Court considered that:

Where an individual has an arguable claim that he has been ill-treated in breach of Article 3, the notion of an effective remedy entails, in addition to a thorough and effective investigation of the kind as also required by Article 3 . . . , effective access for the complainant to the investigatory procedure and payment of compensation where appropriate.[41]

3. The European Committee for the Prevention of Torture and Inhuman or Degrading Treatment or Punishment

39.   In 1987, the Council of Europe adopted the European Convention for the Prevention of Torture and Inhuman or Degrading Treatment or Punishment, which entered into force on 1 February 1989.[42] By 1 March 1999, all 40 member States of the Council of Europe had ratified the Convention. This Convention complements the judicial mechanism of the European Convention on Human Rights with a preventive mechanism. The Convention intentionally does not create substantive norms. The Convention established the European Committee for the Prevention of Torture and Inhuman or Degrading Treatment or Punishment, consisting of one member per member State. The members elected to the Committee should be of high moral standard, impartial, independent and also available to carry out field missions.

40.   The Committee carries out visits to member States of the Council of Europe, partially on a regular periodic basis and partially on an ad hoc basis. A visiting delegation of the Committee consists of members of the Committee, accompanying experts in the medical, legal or other fields, interpreters and members of the secretariat. These delegations visit persons deprived of their liberty by the authorities of the country visited.[43] The powers of each visiting delegation are quite vast: it may visit any place where persons are held deprived of their liberty; make unannounced visits to any such place; repeat visits to these places; talk to persons deprived of their liberty in private; visit any or all persons it chooses to in these places; and see all premises (not only cell areas) without restrictions. The delegation can have access to all papers and files concerning the persons visited. The entire work of the Committee is based on confidentiality and cooperation.

41.   After a visit, the Committee writes a report. Based on the facts observed during the visit, the report comments on the conditions found, makes concrete recommendations and asks any questions that need further clarification. The State party answers the report in writing and thereby establishes a dialogue between the Committee and the State party, which continues until the following visit. The Committee's reports and the State party's answers are confidential documents, but the State party

(not the Committee) may decide to publish both the reports and the answers. So far, nearly all the States parties have made public both reports and answers.

42.   In the course of its activities over the past 10 years, the Committee has gradually developed a set of criteria for the treatment of persons held in custody that constitutes general standards. These standards deal not only with the material conditions but also with procedural safeguards. For example, three safeguards advocated by the Committee for persons held in police custody are:

(a)   The right of a person deprived of liberty, if he or she so desires, to inform immediately a third party (family member) of the arrest;

(b)   The right of a person deprived of liberty to have immediate access to a lawyer;

(c)   The right of a person deprived of liberty to have access to a physician, including, if he or she so wishes, a physician of his or her own choice.

43.   Furthermore, the Committee has stressed repeatedly that one of the most effective means of preventing ill-treatment by law enforcement officials lies in the diligent examination by competent authorities of all complaints of such treatment brought before them and, where appropriate, the imposition of a suitable penalty. This has a strong dissuasive effect.

4. The African Commission on Human and Peoples' Rights and the African Court on Human and Peoples' Rights

44.   In comparison with the European and inter-American systems, Africa does not have a convention on torture and its prevention. The question of torture is examined on the same level as are other human rights violations. The question of torture is dealt with primarily in the African Charter of Human and Peoples' Rights, which was adopted by the Organization of African Unity on 27 June 1981 and which entered into force on 21 October 1986.[44] Article 5 of the African Charter states:

Every individual shall have the right to the respect of the dignity inherent in a human being and to the recognition of his legal status. All forms of exploitation and degradation of man particularly slavery, slave trade, torture, cruel, inhuman or degrading punishment and treatment shall be prohibited.

45.   In accordance with article 30 of the African Charter, the African Commission on Human and Peoples' Rights was established in June 1987 and was charged "to promote human and peoples' rights and ensure their protection in Africa". In its periodic sessions, the Commission has passed several country resolutions on matters concerning human rights in Africa, some of which have dealt with torture, among other violations. In some of its country resolutions, the Commission raised concerns about the degradation of human rights situations, including the practice of torture.

---

[41] Ibid., para. 117.

[42] *European Treaty Series,* No. 126.

[43] A person deprived of liberty is any person deprived of liberty by a public authority, such as, but not exclusively, persons arrested or in any form of detention, prisoners awaiting trial, sentenced prisoners and persons involuntarily confined to psychiatric hospitals.

[44] Organization of African Unity, document CAB/LEG/67/3, Rev. 5, 21, *International Legal Materials,* 58 (1982).

46. The Commission has established new mechanisms, such as the Special Rapporteur on Prisons, the Special Rapporteur on Arbitrary and Summary Executions and the Special Rapporteur on Women, whose mandate is to report during the open sessions of the Commission. These mechanisms have created opportunities for victims and NGOs to send information directly to special rapporteurs. At the same time, a victim or an NGO can make a complaint to the Commission regarding acts of torture as defined in article 5 of the African Charter. While an individual complaint is pending before the Commission, the victim or the NGO can send the same information to special rapporteurs for their public reports to the Commission's sessions. To provide a forum for adjudicating claims of violations of the rights guaranteed in the African Charter, the Organization of African Unity Assembly adopted a protocol for the establishment of the African Court of Human and Peoples' Rights in June 1998.

D. The International Criminal Court

47. The Rome Statute of the International Criminal Court, adopted on 17 July 1998, established a permanent international criminal court to try individuals responsible for genocide, crimes against humanity and war crimes (A/CONF.183/9). The Court has jurisdiction over cases alleging torture either as part of the crime of genocide or as a crime against humanity, if the torture is committed as part of a widespread or systematic attack, or as a war crime under the Geneva Conventions of 1949. Torture is defined in the Rome Statute as the intentional infliction of severe pain or suffering, whether physical or mental, upon a person in the custody or under the control of the accused. As of 25 September 2000, the Rome Statute of the International Criminal Court had been signed by 113 countries and ratified by 21 States. The Court will have its headquarters in The Hague. This Court has jurisdiction only in cases in which States are unable or unwilling to prosecute individuals responsible for the crimes described in the Rome Statute.

CHAPTER II

RELEVANT ETHICAL CODES

48.   All professions work within ethical codes, which provide a statement of the shared values and acknowledged duties of professionals and set moral standards with which they are expected to comply. Ethical standards are established primarily in two ways: by international instruments drawn up by bodies like the United Nations and by codes of principles drafted by the professions themselves, through their representative associations, nationally or internationally. The fundamental tenets are invariably the same and focus on obligations owed by the professional to individual clients or patients, to society at large and to colleagues in order to maintain the honour of the profession. These obligations reflect and complement the rights to which all people are entitled under international instruments.

A.   Ethics of the legal profession

49.   As the ultimate arbiters of justice, judges play a special role in the protection of the rights of citizens. International standards create an ethical duty on the part of judges to ensure that the rights of individuals are protected. Principle 6 of the United Nations Basic Principles on the Independence of the Judiciary states that "The principle of the independence of the judiciary entitles and requires the judiciary to ensure that judicial proceedings are conducted fairly and that the rights of the parties are respected".[45] Similarly, prosecutors have an ethical duty to investigate and prosecute a crime of torture committed by public officials. Article 15 of the United Nations Guidelines on the Role of Prosecutors states: "Prosecutors shall give due attention to the prosecution of crimes committed by public officials, particularly corruption, abuse of power, grave violations of human rights and other crimes recognized by international law and, where authorized by law or consistent with local practice, the investigation of such offences."[46]

50.   International standards also establish a duty for lawyers, in carrying out their professional functions, to promote and protect human rights and fundamental freedoms. Principle 14 of the United Nations Basic Principles on the Role of Lawyers provides: "Lawyers, in protecting the rights of their clients and in promoting the cause of justice, shall seek to uphold human rights and fundamental freedoms recognized by national and international law and shall at all times act freely and diligently in accordance with the law and recognized standards and ethics of the legal profession."[47]

B.   Health-care ethics

51.   There are very clear links between concepts of human rights and the well-established principle of health-care ethics. The ethical obligations of health professionals are articulated at three levels and are reflected in United Nations documents in the same way as they are for the legal profession. They are also embodied in statements issued by international organizations representing health professionals, such as the World Medical Association, the World Psychiatric Association and the International Council of Nurses.[48] National medical associations and nursing organizations also issue codes of ethics, which their members are expected to follow. The central tenet of all health-care ethics, however articulated, is the fundamental duty always to act in the best interests of the patient, regardless of other constraints, pressures or contractual obligations. In some countries, medical ethical principles, such as that of doctor-patient confidentiality, are incorporated into national law. Even where ethical principles are not established in law in this way, all health professionals are morally bound by the standards set by their professional bodies. They are judged to be guilty of misconduct if they deviate from professional standards without reasonable justification.

1.   *United Nations statements relevant to health professionals*

52.   Health professionals, like all other persons working in prison systems, must observe the Standard Minimum Rules for the Treatment of Prisoners, which require that medical, including psychiatric, services must be

---

[45] Adopted by the Seventh United Nations Congress on the Prevention of Crime and the Treatment of Offenders, held at Milan, Italy, from 26 August to 6 September 1985 and endorsed by General Assembly resolutions 40/32 of 29 November 1985 and 40/146 of 13 December 1985.

[46] Adopted by the Eighth United Nations Congress on the Prevention of Crime and the Treatment of Offenders, held in Havana from 27 August to 7 September 1990.

[47] See footnote 46 above.

[48] There are also a number of regional groupings, such as the Commonwealth Medical Association and the International Conference of Islamic Medical Associations that issue important statements on medical ethics and human rights for their members.

available to all prisoners without discrimination and that all sick prisoners or those requesting treatment be seen daily.[49] These requirements reinforce the ethical obligations of physicians, discussed below, to treat and act in the best interests of patients for whom they have a duty to care. In addition, the United Nations has specifically addressed the ethical obligations of doctors and other health professionals in the Principles of Medical Ethics relevant to the Role of Health Personnel, particularly Physicians, in the Protection of Prisoners and Detainees against Torture and Other Cruel, Inhuman or Degrading Treatment or Punishment.[50] These make clear that health professionals have a moral duty to protect the physical and mental health of detainees. They are specifically prohibited from using medical knowledge and skills in any manner that contravenes international statements of individual rights.[51] In particular, it is a gross contravention of health-care ethics to participate, actively or passively, in torture or condone it in any way.

53.   "Participation in torture" includes evaluating an individual's capacity to withstand ill-treatment; being present at, supervising or inflicting maltreatment; resuscitating individuals for the purposes of further maltreatment or providing medical treatment immediately before, during or after torture on the instructions of those likely to be responsible for it; providing professional knowledge or individuals' personal health information to torturers; and intentionally neglecting evidence and falsifying reports, such as autopsy reports and death certificates.[52] The United Nations Principles also incorporate one of the fundamental rules of health-care ethics by emphasizing that the only ethical relationship between prisoners and health professionals is one designed to evaluate, protect and improve prisoners' health. Thus, assessment of detainees' health in order to facilitate punishment or torture is clearly unethical.

2.   *Statements from international professional bodies*

54.   Many statements from international professional bodies focus on principles relevant to the protection of human rights and represent a clear international medical consensus on these issues. Declarations of the World Medical Association define internationally agreed aspects of the ethical duties to which all doctors are held. The World Medical Association's Declaration of Tokyo[53] reiterates the prohibition of any form of medical participation or medical presence in torture or ill-treatment. This is reinforced by the United Nations Principles that specifically refer to the Declaration of Tokyo. Doctors are

clearly prohibited from providing information or any medical instrument or substance that would facilitate ill-treatment. The same rule is specifically applied to psychiatry in the World Psychiatric Association's Declaration of Hawaii,[54] which prohibits the misuse of psychiatric skills to violate the human rights of any individual or group. The International Conference on Islamic Medicine made a similar point in its Declaration of Kuwait,[55] which bans doctors from allowing their special knowledge to be used "to harm, destroy or inflict damage on the body, mind or spirit, whatever the military or political reason". Similar provisions are made for nurses in the directive on the Nurse's Role in the Care of Detainees and Prisoners.[56]

55.   Health professionals also have a duty to support colleagues who speak out against human rights violations. Failure to do so risks not only an infringement of patient rights and a contravention of the declarations listed above but also brings the health professions into disrepute. Tarnishing the honour of the profession is considered to be serious professional misconduct. The World Medical Association's resolution on human rights[57] calls on all national medical associations to review the human rights situation in their own countries and ensure that doctors do not conceal evidence of abuse even where they fear reprisal. It requires national bodies to provide clear guidance, especially for doctors working in the prison system, to protest alleged violations of human rights and provide effective machinery for investigating doctors' unethical activities in the human rights sphere. It also requires that they support individual doctors who call attention to human rights abuses. The World Medical Association's subsequent Declaration of Hamburg[58] reaffirms the responsibility of individuals and organized medical groups worldwide to encourage doctors to resist torture or any pressure to act contrary to ethical principles. It calls upon individual doctors to speak out against maltreatment and urges national and international medical organizations to support doctors who resist such pressure.

3.   *National codes of medical ethics*

56.   The third level at which ethical principles are articulated is through national codes. These reflect the same core values as mentioned above, since medical ethics are the expression of values common to all doctors. In virtually all cultures and codes, the same basic presumptions occur about duties to avoid harm, help the sick, protect the vulnerable and not discriminate between patients on any basis other than the urgency of their medical needs. Identical values are present in the codes for the nursing profession. A problematic aspect of ethical principles is that they do not, however, provide definitive rules for every dilemma but require some interpretation. When weighing ethical dilemmas, it is vital that health professionals bear in mind the fundamental moral

---

[49] Standard Minimum Rules for the Treatment of Prisoners and Procedures for the Effective Implementation of the Standard Minimum Rules, adopted by the United Nations in 1955.

[50] Adopted by the General Assembly in 1982.

[51] Particularly the Universal Declaration of Human Rights, the International Covenants on Human Rights and the Declaration on the Protection of All Persons from Being Subjected to Torture and Other Cruel, Inhuman or Degrading Treatment or Punishment.

[52] Health professionals must, however, bear in mind the duty of confidentiality owed to patients and the obligation to obtain informed consent for disclosure of information, particularly when individuals may be put at risk by such disclosure (see chapter II, sect. C.3).

[53] Adopted by the World Medical Association in 1975.

[54] Adopted in 1977.

[55] Adopted in 1981 (1401 in the Islamic calendar).

[56] Adopted by the International Council of Nurses in 1975.

[57] Adopted in 1990.

[58] Adopted in 1997.

obligations expressed in their shared professional values but also that they implement them in a manner that reflects the basic duty to avoid harm to their patients.

C. Principles common to all codes of health-care ethics

57. The principle of professional independence requires health professionals always to concentrate on the core purpose of medicine, which is to alleviate suffering and distress and avoid harm, despite other pressures. Several other ethical principles are so fundamental that they are invariably found in all codes and ethical statements. The most basic are the injunctions to provide compassionate care, do no harm and to respect patients' rights. These are central requirements for all health professionals.

1. *The duty to provide compassionate care*

58. The duty to provide care is expressed in a variety of ways in national and international codes and declarations. One aspect of this duty is the medical duty to respond to those in medical need. This is reflected in the World Medical Association's International Code of Medical Ethics,[59] which recognizes the moral obligation of doctors to provide emergency care as a humanitarian duty. The duty to respond to need and suffering is echoed in traditional statements in virtually all cultures.

59. Underpinning much of modern medical ethics are the principles established in the earliest statements of professional values that require doctors to provide care even at some risk to themselves. For example, the Caraka Samhita, a Hindu code dating from the first century AD, instructs doctors to "endeavour for the relief of patients with all thy heart and soul. Thou shall not desert or injure thy patient for the sake of thy life or thy living". Similar instructions were given in early Islamic codes and the modern Declaration of Kuwait requires doctors to focus on the needy, be they "near or far, virtuous or sinner, friend or enemy".

60. Western medical values have been dominated by the influence of the Hippocratic oath and similar pledges, such as the Prayer of Maimonides. The Hippocratic oath represents a solemn promise of solidarity with other doctors and a commitment to benefit and care for patients while avoiding harming them. It also contains a promise to maintain confidentiality. These four concepts are reflected in various forms in all modern professional codes of health-care ethics. The World Medical Association's Declaration of Geneva[60] is a modern restatement of the Hippocratic values. It is a promise by which doctors undertake to make the health of their patients their primary consideration and vow to devote themselves to the service of humanity with conscience and dignity.

61. Aspects of the duty to care are reflected in many of the World Medical Association's declarations, which make clear that doctors must always do what is best for the patient, including detainees and alleged criminals. This duty is often expressed through the notion of professional independence, requiring doctors to adhere to best medical practices despite any pressure that might be applied. The World Medical Association's International Code of Medical Ethics emphasizes doctors' duty to provide care "in full technical and moral independence, with compassion and respect for human dignity". It also stresses the duty to act only in the patient's interest and says that doctors owe their patients complete loyalty. The World Medical Association's Tokyo Declaration and Declaration on Physician Independence and Professional Freedom[61] make unambiguously clear that doctors must insist on being free to act in patients' interests, regardless of other considerations, including the instructions of employers, prison authorities or security forces. The latter declaration requires doctors to ensure that they "have the professional independence to represent and defend the health needs of patients against all who would deny or restrict needed care for those who are sick or injured". Similar principles are prescribed for nurses in the International Council of Nurses Code of Ethics.

62. Another way in which duty to provide care is expressed by the World Medical Association is through its recognition of patient rights. Its Declaration of Lisbon on the Rights of the Patient[62] recognizes that every person is entitled, without discrimination, to appropriate health care and reiterates that doctors must always act in a patient's best interest. Patients must be guaranteed autonomy and justice, according to the Declaration, and both doctors and providers of medical care must uphold patient's rights. "Whenever legislation, government action or any other administration or institution denies patients these rights, physicians should pursue appropriate means to assure or to restore them." Individuals are entitled to appropriate health care, regardless of factors such as their ethnic origin, political beliefs, nationality, gender, religion or individual merit. People accused or convicted of crimes have an equal moral entitlement to appropriate medical and nursing care. The World Medical Association's Declaration of Lisbon emphasizes that the only acceptable criterion for discriminating between patients is the relative urgency of their medical need.

2. *Informed consent*

63. While the declarations reflecting a duty of care all emphasize an obligation to act in the best interests of the individual being examined or treated, this presupposes that health professionals know what is in the patient's best interest. An absolutely fundamental precept of modern medical ethics is that patients themselves are the best judge of their own interests. This requires health professionals to give normal precedence to a competent adult patient's wishes rather than to the views of any person in authority about what would be best for that individual. Where the patient is unconscious or otherwise incapable of giving valid consent, health professionals must make a judgement about how that person's best interests can be

---

[59] Adopted in 1949.
[60] Adopted in 1948.

[61] Adopted by the World Medical Association in 1986.
[62] Adopted by the World Medical Association in 1981; amended by its General Assembly at its forty-seventh session in September 1995.

protected and promoted. Nurses and doctors are expected to act as an advocate for their patients, and this is made clear in statements such as the World Medical Association's Declaration of Lisbon and the International Council of Nurses' statement on the Nurse's Role in Safeguarding Human Rights.[63]

64. The World Medical Association's Declaration of Lisbon specifies the duty for doctors to obtain voluntary and informed consent from mentally competent patients to any examination or procedure. This means that individuals need to know the implications of agreeing and the consequences of refusing. Before examining patients, health professionals must, therefore, explain frankly the purpose of the examination and treatment. Consent obtained under duress or as a result of false information being given to the patient is invalid, and doctors acting on it are likely to be in breach of medical ethics. The graver the implications of the procedure for the patient, the greater the moral imperative to obtain properly informed consent. That is to say, where examination and treatment are clearly of therapeutic benefit to individuals, their implied consent by cooperating in the procedures may be sufficient. In cases where examination is not primarily for the purposes of providing therapeutic care, great caution is required in ensuring that the patient knows and agrees to this and that it is in no way contrary to the individual's best interests. As previously stated, examination to ascertain whether an individual can withstand punishment, torture or physical pressure during interrogation is unethical and contrary to the purpose of medicine. The only ethical assessment of a prisoner's health is one designed to evaluate the patient's health in order to maintain and improve optimum health, not to facilitate punishment. Physical examination for evidential purposes in an inquiry requires consent that is informed in the sense that the patient understands factors such as how the health data gained from the examination will be used, how they will be stored and who will have access to them. If these and other points relevant to the patient's decision are not made clear in advance, consent to examination and recording of information is invalid.

3. *Confidentiality*

65. All ethical codes, from the Hippocratic oath to modern times, include the duty of confidentiality as a fundamental principle, which also features prominently in the World Medical Association's declarations, such as the Declaration of Lisbon. In some jurisdictions, the obligation of professional secrecy is seen as so important that it is incorporated into national law. The duty of confidentiality is not absolute and may be ethically breached in exceptional circumstances where failure to do so will foreseeably give rise to serious harm to people or a serious perversion of justice. Generally, however, the duty of confidentiality covering identifiable personal health information can be overridden only with the informed permission of the patient.[64] Non-identifiable patient information can be freely used for other purposes and

should be used preferably in all situations where disclosure of the patient's identity is non-essential. This may be the case, for example, in the collection of data about patterns of torture or maltreatment. Dilemmas arise where health professionals are pressured or required by law to disclose identifiable information which would be likely to put patients at risk of harm. In such cases, the fundamental ethical obligations are to respect the autonomy and best interests of the patient, to do good and avoid harm. This supersedes other considerations. Doctors should make clear to the court or the authority requesting information that they are bound by professional duties of confidentiality. Health professionals responding in this way are entitled to the support of their professional association and colleagues. In addition, during periods of armed conflict, international humanitarian law gives specific protection to doctor-patient confidentiality, requiring that doctors do not denounce people who are sick or wounded.[65] Health professionals are protected in that they cannot be compelled to disclose information about their patients in such situations.

D. Health professionals with dual obligations

66. Health professionals have dual obligations, in that they owe a primary duty to the patient to promote that person's best interests and a general duty to society to ensure that justice is done and violations of human rights prevented. Dilemmas arising from these dual obligations are particularly acute for health professionals working with the police, military, other security services or in the prison system. The interests of their employer and their non-medical colleagues may be in conflict with the best interests of the detainee patients. Whatever the circumstances of their employment, all health professionals owe a fundamental duty to care for the people they are asked to examine or treat. They cannot be obliged by contractual or other considerations to compromise their professional independence. They must make an unbiased assessment of the patient's health interests and act accordingly.

1. *Principles guiding all doctors with dual obligations*

67. In all cases where doctors are acting for another party, they have an obligation to ensure that this is understood by the patient.[66] Doctors must identify themselves to patients and explain the purpose of any examination or treatment. Even when doctors are appointed and paid by a third party, they retain a clear duty of care to any patient whom they examine or treat. They must refuse to comply with any procedures that may harm patients or leave them physically or psychologically vulnerable to harm. They must ensure that their contractual terms allow them professional independence to make clinical judgements. Doctors must ensure that any person in custody has access to any medical examination and treatment needed. Where the detainee is a minor or a vulnerable adult, doctors have additional duties to act as an advocate. Doctors retain a

---

[63] Adopted in 1983.

[64] Except for common public health requirements, such as the reporting by name of individuals with infectious diseases, drug addiction, mental disorders, etc.

[65] Article 16 of Protocol I (1977) and article 10 of Protocol II (1977), additional to the Geneva Conventions of 1949.

[66] These principles are extracted from *Doctors with Dual Obligations* (London, British Medical Association, 1995).

general duty of confidentiality so that information should not be disclosed without the patient's knowledge. They must ensure that their medical records are kept confidential. Doctors have a duty to monitor and speak out when services in which they are involved are unethical, abusive, inadequate or pose a potential threat to patients' health. In such cases, they have an ethical duty to take prompt action as failure to take an immediate stand makes protest at a later stage more difficult. They should report the matter to appropriate authorities or international agencies who can investigate, but without exposing patients, their families or themselves to foreseeable serious risk of harm. Doctors and professional associations should support colleagues who take such action on the basis of reasonable evidence.

2. *Dilemmas arising from dual obligations*

68. Dilemmas may occur when ethics and law are in contradiction. Circumstances can arise where their ethical duties oblige health professionals not to obey a particular law, such as a legal obligation to reveal confidential medical information about a patient. There is consensus in international and national declarations of ethical precepts that other imperatives, including the law, cannot oblige health professionals to act contrary to medical ethics and to their conscience. In such cases, health professionals must decline to comply with the law or a regulation rather than compromise basic ethical precepts or expose patients to serious danger.

69. In some cases, two ethical obligations are in conflict. International codes and ethical principles require the reporting of information concerning torture or maltreatment to a responsible body. In some jurisdictions, this is also a legal requirement. In some cases, however, patients may refuse to give consent to being examined for such purposes or to having the information gained from examination disclosed to others. They may be fearful of the risks of reprisals for themselves or their families. In such situations, health professionals have dual responsibilities: to the patient and to society at large, which has an interest in ensuring that justice is done and perpetrators of abuse are brought to justice. The fundamental principle of avoiding harm must feature prominently in consideration of such dilemmas. Health professionals should seek solutions that promote justice without breaching the individual's right to confidentiality. Advice should be sought from reliable agencies; in some cases this may be the national medical association or non-governmental agencies. Alternatively, with supportive encouragement, some reluctant patients may agree to disclosure within agreed parameters.

70. The ethical obligations of a doctor may vary according to the context of the doctor-patient encounter and the possibility of the patient being able to exercise free choice about the disclosure decision. For example, where the doctor and patient are in a clearly therapeutic situation, such as the provision of care in hospital, there is a strong moral imperative for doctors to preserve the usual rules of confidentiality that normally prevail in therapeutic relationships. Reporting evidence of torture obtained in such encounters is entirely appropriate as long as the patient does not forbid it. Doctors should report such

evidence if patients request it or give properly informed consent to it. They should support patients in such decisions.

71. Forensic doctors have a different relationship with the individuals they examine and usually have an obligation to report their observations factually. The patient has less power and choice in such situations and may not be able to speak openly about what has occurred. Before beginning any examination, forensic doctors must explain their role to the patient and make clear that medical confidentiality is not a usual part of their role, as it would be in a therapeutic context. Regulations may not permit the patient to refuse examination, but the patient has an option of choosing whether to disclose the cause of any injury. Forensic doctors should not falsify their reports but should provide impartial evidence, including making clear in their reports any evidence of maltreatment.[67]

72. Prison doctors are primarily providers of therapeutic treatment but they also have the task of examining detainees arriving in prison from police custody. In this role or in treatment of people within a prison, they may discover evidence of unacceptable violence, which prisoners themselves are not in a realistic position to denounce. In such situations, doctors must bear in mind the best interests of the patient and their duties of confidentiality to that person, but the moral arguments for the doctor to denounce evident maltreatment are strong, since prisoners themselves are often unable to do so effectively. Where prisoners agree to disclosure, no conflict arises and the moral obligation is clear. If a prisoner refuses to allow disclosure, doctors must weigh the risk and potential danger to that individual patient against the benefits to the general prison population and the interests of society in preventing the perpetuation of abuse.

73. Health professionals must also bear in mind that reporting abuse to the authorities in whose jurisdiction it is alleged to have occurred may well entail risks of harm for the patient or for others, including the whistle-blower. Doctors must not knowingly place individuals in danger of reprisal. They are not exempt from taking action but should use discretion and must consider reporting the information to a responsible body outside the immediate jurisdiction or, where this would not entail foreseeable risks to health professionals and patients, report it in a non-identifiable manner. Clearly, if the latter solution is taken, health professionals must take into account the likelihood of pressure being brought on them to disclose identifying data or the possibility of having their medical records forcibly seized. While there are no easy solutions, health professionals should be guided by the basic injunction to avoid harm above all other considerations and seek advice, where possible, from national or international medical bodies.

---

[67] See V. Iacopino and others, "Physician complicity in misrepresentation and omission of evidence of torture in postdetention medical examinations in Turkey", *Journal of the American Medical Association (JAMA)*, vol. 276 (1996), pp. 396-402.

CHAPTER III

LEGAL INVESTIGATION OF TORTURE

74. States are required under international law to investigate reported incidents of torture promptly and impartially. Where evidence warrants it, a State in whose territory a person alleged to have committed or participated in torture is present, must either extradite the alleged perpetrator to another State that has competent jurisdiction or submit the case to its own competent authorities for the purpose of prosecution under national or local criminal laws. The fundamental principles of any viable investigation into incidents of torture are competence, impartiality, independence, promptness and thoroughness. These elements can be adapted to any legal system and should guide all investigations of alleged torture.

75. Where investigative procedures are inadequate because of a lack of resources or expertise, the appearance of bias, the apparent existence of a pattern of abuse or other substantial reasons, States shall pursue investigations through an independent commission of inquiry or similar procedure. Members of that commission must be chosen for their recognized impartiality, competence and independence as individuals. In particular, they must be independent of any institution, agency or person that may be the subject of the inquiry.

76. Section A describes the broad purpose of an investigation into torture. Section B sets forth basic principles on the effective investigation and documentation of torture and other cruel, inhuman or degrading treatment or punishment. Section C sets forth suggested procedures for conducting an investigation into alleged torture, first considering the decision regarding the appropriate investigative authority, then offering guidelines regarding collection of oral testimony from the reported victim and other witnesses and collection of physical evidence. Section D provides guidelines for establishing a special independent commission of inquiry. These guidelines are based on the experiences of several countries that have established independent commissions to investigate alleged human rights abuses, including extrajudicial killings, torture and disappearances.

A. Purposes of an investigation into torture

77. The broad purpose of the investigation is to establish the facts relating to alleged incidents of torture, with a view to identifying those responsible for the incidents and facilitating their prosecution, or for use in the context of other procedures designed to obtain redress for victims. The issues addressed here may also be relevant

for other types of investigations of torture. To fulfil this purpose, those carrying out the investigation must, at a minimum, seek to obtain statements from the victims of alleged torture; to recover and preserve evidence, including medical evidence, related to the alleged torture to aid in any potential prosecution of those responsible; to identify possible witnesses and obtain statements from them concerning the alleged torture; and to determine how, when and where the alleged incidents of torture occurred as well as any pattern or practice that may have brought about the torture.

B. Principles on the Effective Investigation and Documentation of Torture and Other Cruel, Inhuman or Degrading Treatment or Punishment

78. The following principles represent a consensus among individuals and organizations having expertise in the investigation of torture. The purposes of effective investigation and documentation of torture and other cruel, inhuman or degrading treatment or punishment (hereinafter referred to as torture or other ill-treatment) include the following:

(a) Clarification of the facts and establishment and acknowledgement of individual and State responsibility for victims and their families;

(b) Identification of measures needed to prevent recurrence;

(c) Facilitation of prosecution or, as appropriate, disciplinary sanctions for those indicated by the investigation as being responsible and demonstration of the need for full reparation and redress from the State, including fair and adequate financial compensation and provision of the means for medical care and rehabilitation.

79. States must ensure that complaints and reports of torture or ill-treatment are promptly and effectively investigated. Even in the absence of an express complaint, an investigation should be undertaken if there are other indications that torture or ill-treatment might have occurred. The investigators, who shall be independent of the suspected perpetrators and the agency they serve, must be competent and impartial. They must have access to or be empowered to commission investigations by impartial medical or other experts. The methods used to carry out these investigations must meet the highest professional standards, and the findings must be made public.

80. The investigative authority shall have the power and obligation to obtain all the information necessary to the inquiry.[68] The persons conducting the investigation must have at their disposal all the necessary budgetary and technical resources for effective investigation. They must also have the authority to oblige all those acting in an official capacity allegedly involved in torture or ill-treatment to appear and testify. The same applies to any witness. To this end, the investigative authority is entitled to issue summonses to witnesses, including any officials allegedly involved, and to demand the production of evidence. Alleged victims of torture or ill-treatment, witnesses, those conducting the investigation and their families must be protected from violence, threats of violence or any other form of intimidation that may arise pursuant to the investigation. Those potentially implicated in torture or ill-treatment should be removed from any position of control or power, whether direct or indirect, over complainants, witnesses or their families, as well as those conducting the investigation.

81. Alleged victims of torture or ill-treatment and their legal representatives must be informed of, and have access to, any hearing as well as to all information relevant to the investigation and must be entitled to present other evidence.

82. In cases in which the established investigative procedures are inadequate because of insufficient expertise or suspected bias, or because of the apparent existence of a pattern of abuse, or for other substantial reasons, States must ensure that investigations are undertaken through an independent commission of inquiry or similar procedure. Members of such a commission should be chosen for their recognized impartiality, competence and independence as individuals. In particular, they must be independent of any suspected perpetrators and the institutions or agencies they may serve. The commission must have the authority to obtain all information necessary to the inquiry and shall conduct the inquiry as provided for under these principles.[69] A written report, made within a reasonable time, must include the scope of the inquiry, procedures and methods used to evaluate evidence as well as conclusions and recommendations based on findings of fact and on applicable law. On completion, this report must be made public. It must also describe in detail specific events that were found to have occurred, the evidence upon which such findings were based and list the names of witnesses who testified with the exception of those whose identities have been withheld for their own protection. The State must, within a reasonable period of time, reply to the report of the investigation and, as appropriate, indicate steps to be taken in response.

83. Medical experts involved in the investigation of torture or ill-treatment should behave at all times in conformity with the highest ethical standards and, in particular, must obtain informed consent before any examination is undertaken. The examination must conform to established standards of medical practice. In particular, examinations must be conducted in private under the control of the medical expert and outside the presence of security agents and other government officials. The medical expert should promptly prepare an accurate written report. This report should include at least the following:

(a) The circumstances of the interview. The name of the subject and name and affiliation of those present at the examination; the exact time and date, location, nature and address of the institution (including, where appropriate, the room) where the examination is being conducted (e.g. detention centre, clinic, house, etc.); any appropriate circumstances at the time of the examination (e.g. nature of any restraints on arrival or during the examination, presence of security forces during the examination, demeanour of those accompanying the prisoner, threatening statements to the examiner, etc.); and any other relevant factor;

(b) The background. A detailed record of the subject's story as given during the interview, including alleged methods of torture or ill-treatment, the time when torture or ill-treatment was alleged to have occurred and all complaints of physical and psychological symptoms;

(c) A physical and psychological examination. A record of all physical and psychological findings upon clinical examination including appropriate diagnostic tests and, where possible, colour photographs of all injuries;

(d) An opinion. An interpretation as to the probable relationship of physical and psychological findings to possible torture or ill-treatment. A recommendation for any necessary medical and psychological treatment or further examination should also be given;

(e) A record of authorship. The report should clearly identify those carrying out the examination and should be signed.

84. The report should be confidential and communicated to the subject or his or her nominated representative. The views of the subject and his or her representative about the examination process should be solicited and recorded in the report. The report should be provided in writing, where appropriate, to the authority responsible for investigating the allegation of torture or ill-treatment. It is the responsibility of the State to ensure that the report is delivered securely to these persons. The report should not be made available to any other person, except with the consent of the subject or when authorized by a court empowered to enforce the transfer. For general considerations for written reports following allegations of torture, see chapter IV. Chapters V and VI describe in detail the physical and psychological assessments, respectively.

C. Procedures of a torture investigation

1. *Determination of the appropriate investigative body*

85. In cases where involvement in torture by public officials is suspected, including possible orders for the use of torture by ministers, ministerial aides, officers acting with the knowledge of ministers, senior officers in State ministries, senior military leaders or tolerance of torture by such individuals, an objective and impartial investigation may not be possible unless a special commission of inquiry is established. A commission of inquiry may also

---

[68] Under certain circumstances professional ethics may require information to be kept confidential. These requirements should be respected.

[69] See footnote 68.

be necessary where the expertise or the impartiality of the investigators is called into question.

86. Factors that support a belief that the State was involved in the torture or that special circumstances exist that should trigger the creation of a special impartial investigation mechanism include:

(a) Where the victim was last seen unharmed in police custody or detention;

(b) Where the modus operandi is recognizably attributable to State-sponsored torture;

(c) Where persons in the State or associated with the State have attempted to obstruct or delay the investigation of the torture;

(d) Where public interest would be served by an independent inquiry;

(e) Where investigation by regular investigative agencies is in question because of lack of expertise or lack of impartiality or for other reasons, including the importance of the matter, the apparent existence of a pattern of abuse, complaints from the person or the above inadequacies or other substantial reasons.

87. Several considerations should be taken into account when a State decides to establish an independent commission of inquiry. First, persons subject to an inquiry should be guaranteed the minimum procedural safeguards protected by international law at all stages of the investigation. Second, investigators should have the support of adequate technical and administrative personnel, as well as access to objective, impartial legal advice to ensure that the investigation will produce admissible evidence for criminal proceedings. Third, investigators should receive the full scope of the State's resources and powers. Finally, investigators should have the power to seek help from the international community of experts in law and medicine.

2. *Interviewing the alleged victim and other witnesses*

88. Because of the nature of torture cases and the trauma individuals suffer as a result, often including a devastating sense of powerlessness, it is particularly important to show sensitivity to the alleged torture victim and other witnesses. The State must protect alleged victims of torture, witnesses and their families from violence, threats of violence or any other form of intimidation that may arise pursuant to the investigation. Investigators must inform witnesses about the consequences of their involvement in the investigation and about any subsequent developments in the case that may affect them.

(a) *Informed consent and other protection for the alleged victim*

89. From the outset, the alleged victim should be informed, wherever possible, of the nature of the proceedings, why his or her evidence is being sought, if and how evidence offered by the alleged victim may be used. Investigators should explain to the person which portions of the investigation will be public information and which portions will be confidential. The person has the right to refuse to cooperate with all or part of the investigation.

Every effort should be made to accommodate his or her schedule and wishes. The alleged torture victim should be regularly informed of the progress of the investigation. The alleged victim should also be notified of all key hearings in the investigation and prosecution of the case. The investigators should inform the alleged victim of the arrest of the suspected perpetrator. Alleged victims of torture should be given contact information for advocacy and treatment groups that might be of assistance to them. Investigators should work with advocacy groups within their jurisdiction to ensure that there is a mutual exchange of information and training concerning torture.

(b) *Selection of the investigator*

90. The authorities investigating the case must identify a person primarily responsible for questioning the alleged victim. While the alleged victim may need to discuss his or her case with both legal and medical professionals, the investigating team should make every effort to minimize unnecessary repetitions of the person's story. In selecting a person as the primary investigator with responsibility for the alleged torture victim, special consideration should be given to the victim's preference for a person of the same gender, the same cultural background or the ability to communicate in his or her native language. The primary investigator should have prior training or experience in documenting torture and in working with victims of trauma, including torture. In situations where an investigator with prior training or experience is not available, the primary investigator should make every effort to become informed about torture and its physical and psychological consequences before interviewing the individual. Information about torture is available from sources including this manual, several professional and training publications, training courses and professional conferences. The investigator should also have access to international expert advice and assistance throughout the investigation.

(c) *Context of the investigation*

91. Investigators should carefully consider the context in which they are working, take necessary precautions and provide safeguards accordingly. If interviewing people who are still imprisoned or in similar situations in which reprisals are possible, the interviewer should use care not to put them in danger. In situations where talking to an investigator may endanger someone, a "group interview" may be preferable to an individual interview. In other cases, the interviewer must choose a place for the private interview where the witness feels comfortable to talk freely.

92. Evaluations occur in a variety of political contexts. This results in important differences in the manner in which evaluations should be conducted. The legal standards under which the investigation is conducted are also affected by the context. For example, an investigation culminating in the trial of an alleged perpetrator will require the highest level of proof, whereas a report supporting an application for political asylum in a third country need provide only a relatively low level of proof of torture. The investigator must adapt the following guidelines according to the particular situation and purpose of the

evaluation. Examples of various contexts include, but are not limited to, the following:

(i) In prison or detention in the individual's home country;

(ii) In prison or detention in another country;

(iii) Not in detention in the home country but in a hostile oppressive climate;

(iv) Not in detention in the home country during a time of peace and security;

(v) In another country that may be friendly or hostile;

(vi) In a refugee camp setting;

(vii) In a war crimes tribunal or truth commission.

93. The political context may be hostile towards the victim and the examiner, for example, when detainees are interviewed while they are held in prison by their governments or while they are detained by foreign governments in order to be deported. In countries where asylum-seekers are examined in order to establish evidence of torture, the reluctance to acknowledge claims of trauma and torture may be politically motivated. The possibility of further endangering the safety of the detainee is very real and must be taken into account during every evaluation. Even in cases where persons alleging torture are not in imminent danger, investigators should use great care in their contact with them. The investigator's choice of language and attitude will greatly affect the alleged victim's ability and willingness to be interviewed. The location of the interview should be as safe and comfortable as possible, including access to toilet facilities and refreshments. Sufficient time should be allotted to interview the alleged torture victim. Investigators should not expect to get the full story during the first interview. Questions of a private nature will be traumatic for the alleged victim. The investigator must be sensitive in tone, phrasing and sequencing of questions, given the traumatic nature of the alleged victim's testimony. The witness must be told of the right to stop the questioning at any time, to take a break if needed or to choose not to respond to any question.

94. Psychological counsellors or those trained in working with torture victims should be accessible, if possible, to the alleged torture victim, witnesses and members of the investigating team. Retelling the facts of the torture may cause the person to relive the experience or suffer other trauma-related symptoms (see chapter IV, sect. H). Hearing details of torture may result in secondary trauma symptoms to interviewers, and they must be encouraged to discuss their reactions with one another, respecting their professional ethical requirements of confidentiality. Wherever possible, this should be with the help of an experienced facilitator. There are two particular risks to be aware of: first, there is a danger that the interviewer may identify with those alleging torture and not be sufficiently challenging of the story; second, the interviewer may become so used to hearing histories of torture that he or she diminishes in his or her own mind the experiences of the person being interviewed.

(d) *Safety of witnesses*

95. The State is responsible for protecting alleged victims, witnesses and their families from violence, threats of violence or any other form of intimidation that may arise pursuant to the investigation. Those potentially implicated in torture should be removed from any position of control or power, whether direct or indirect over complainants, witnesses and their families as well as those conducting investigations. Investigators must give constant consideration to the effect of the investigation on the safety of the person alleging torture and other witnesses.

96. One suggested technique for providing a measure of safety to interviewees, including prisoners in countries in conflict situations, is to write down and keep safe the identities of people visited so that investigators can follow up on the safety of those individuals at a future return visit. Investigators must be allowed to talk to anyone and everyone, freely and in private, and be allowed to repeat the visit to these same persons (thus the need for traceable identities of those interviewed) as the need arises. Not all countries accept these conditions, and investigators may find it difficult to obtain similar guarantees. In cases in which witnesses are likely to be put in danger because of their testimony, the investigator should seek other forms of evidence.

97. Prisoners are in greater potential danger than persons who are not in custody. Prisoners might have different reactions to different situations. In one situation, prisoners may unwittingly put themselves in danger by speaking out too rashly, thinking they are protected by the very presence of the "outside" investigator. This may not be the case. In other situations, investigators may come up against a "wall of silence", as prisoners are far too intimidated to trust anyone, even when offered talks in private. In the latter case, it may be necessary to start with "group interviews", so as to be able to explain clearly the scope and purpose of the investigation and subsequently offer to have interviews in private with those persons who desire to speak. If the fear of reprisals, justified or not, is too great, it may be necessary to interview all prisoners in a given place of custody, so as not to pinpoint any specific person. Where an investigation leads to prosecution or another public truth-telling forum, the investigator should recommend measures to prevent harm to the alleged torture victim by such means as expunging names and other information that identifies the person from the public records or offering the person an opportunity to testify through image or voice-altering devices or closed circuit television. These measures must be consistent with the rights of the accused.

(e) *Use of interpreters*

98. Working through an interpreter when investigating torture is not easy, even with professionals. It will not always be possible to have interpreters on hand for all different dialects and languages, and sometimes it may be necessary to use interpreters from the person's family or cultural group. This is not ideal, as the person may not always feel comfortable talking about the torture experience through people he or she knows. Ideally, the interpreter should be part of the investigating team and knowl-

edgeable about torture issues (see chapters IV, sect. I, and VI, sect. C.2).

(f) *Information to be obtained from the person alleged to have been tortured*

99. The investigator should attempt to obtain as much of the following information as possible through the testimony of the alleged victim (see chapter IV, sect. E):

(i) The circumstances leading up to the torture, including arrest or abduction and detention;

(ii) Approximate dates and times of the torture, including when the last instance of torture occurred. Establishing this information may not be easy, as there may be several places and perpetrators (or groups of perpetrators) involved. Separate stories may have to be recorded about the different places. Expect chronologies to be inaccurate and sometimes even confusing; notions of time are often hard to focus on for someone who has been tortured. Separate stories about different places may be useful when trying to get a global picture of the situation. Survivors will often not know exactly to where they were taken, having been blindfolded or semi-conscious. By putting together converging testimonies, it may be possible to "map out" specific places, methods and even perpetrators;

(iii) A detailed description of the persons involved in the arrest, detention and torture, including whether he or she knew any of them prior to the events relating to the alleged torture, clothing, scars, birthmarks, tattoos, height, weight (the person may be able to describe the torturer in relation to his or her own size), anything unusual about the perpetrator's anatomy, language and accent and whether the perpetrators were intoxicated at any time;

(iv) Contents of what the person was told or asked. This may provide relevant information when trying to identify secret or unacknowledged places of detention;

(v) A description of the usual routine in the place of detention and the pattern of ill-treatment;

(vi) A description of the facts of the torture, including the methods of torture used. This is understandably often difficult, and investigators should not expect to obtain the full story during one interview. It is important to obtain precise information, but questions related to intimate humiliation and assault will be traumatic, often extremely so;

(vii) Whether the individual was sexually assaulted. Most people will tend to answer a question on sexual assault as meaning actual rape or sodomy. Investigators should be sensitive to the fact that verbal assaults, disrobing, groping, lewd or humiliating acts or blows or electric shocks to the genitals are often not taken by the victim as constituting sexual assault. These acts all violate the individual's intimacy and should be considered as being part and parcel of sexual assault. Very often, victims of sexual assault will say nothing or even deny any sexual assault. It is often only on the second or even third visit, if the contact made has been empathic and sensitive to the person's culture and personality, that more of the story will come out;

(viii) Physical injuries sustained in the course of the torture;

(ix) A description of weapons or other physical objects used;

(x) The identity of witnesses to the events involving torture. The investigator must use care in protecting the safety of witnesses and should consider encrypting the identities of witnesses or keeping these names separate from the substantive interview notes.

(g) *Statement from the person who is alleging torture*

100. The investigator should tape-record a detailed statement from the person and have it transcribed. The statement should be based on answers given in response to non-leading questions. Non-leading questions do not make assumptions or conclusions and allow the person to offer the most complete and unbiased testimony. Examples of non-leading questions are "What happened to you and where?" rather than "Were you tortured in prison?". The latter question assumes that what happened to the witness was torture and limits the location of the actions to a prison. Avoid asking questions with lists, as this can force the individual into giving inaccurate answers if what actually happened does not exactly match one of the options. Allow the person to tell his or her own story, but assist by asking questions that increase in specificity. Encourage the person to use all his/her senses in describing what has happened to him or her. Ask what he or she saw, smelled, heard and felt. This is important, for instance, in situations where the person may have been blindfolded or experienced the assault in the dark.

(h) *Alleged perpetrator's statement*

101. If possible, the investigators should interview the alleged perpetrators. The investigators must provide them with legal protections guaranteed under international and national law.

3. *Securing and obtaining physical evidence*

102. The investigator should gather as much physical evidence as possible to document an incident or pattern of torture. One of the most important aspects of a thorough and impartial investigation of torture is the collection and analysis of physical evidence. Investigators should document the chain of custody involved in recovering and preserving physical evidence in order to use such evidence in future legal proceedings, including potential criminal prosecution. Most torture occurs in places where people are held in some form of custody, where preservation of physical evidence or unrestricted access may be initially difficult or even impossible. Investigators must be given authority by the State to obtain unrestricted access to any place or premises and be able to secure the setting where torture allegedly took place. Investigative personnel and other investigators should coordinate their efforts in

carrying out a thorough investigation of the place where torture allegedly occurred. Investigators must have unrestricted access to the alleged scene of torture. Their access must include, but not be limited to, open or closed areas, including buildings, vehicles, offices, prison cells or other premises where torture is alleged to have taken place.

103. Any building or area under investigation must be closed off so as not to lose any possible evidence. Only investigators and their staff should be allowed entry into the area once it has been designated as under investigation. Examination of the scene for any material evidence should take place. All evidence must be properly collected, handled, packaged, labelled and placed in safekeeping to prevent contamination, tampering or loss of evidence. If the torture has allegedly taken place recently enough for such evidence to be relevant, any samples found of body fluids (such as blood or semen), hair, fibres and threads should be collected, labelled and properly preserved. Any implements that could be used to inflict torture, whether they be destined for that purpose or used circumstantially, should be taken and preserved. If recent enough to be relevant, any fingerprints located must be lifted and preserved. A labelled sketch of the premises or place where torture has allegedly taken place must be made to scale, showing all relevant details, such as the location of the floors in a building, rooms, entrances, windows, furniture and surrounding terrain. Colour photographs must also be taken to record the same. A record of the identity of all persons at the alleged torture scene must be made, including complete names, addresses and telephone numbers or other contact information. If torture is recent enough for it to be relevant, an inventory of the clothing of the person alleging torture should be taken and tested at a laboratory, if available, for bodily fluids and other physical evidence. Information must be obtained from anyone present on the premises or in the area under investigation to determine whether they were witness to the incidents of alleged torture. Any relevant papers, records or documents should be saved for evidential use and handwriting analysis.

4. *Medical evidence*

104. The investigator should arrange for a medical examination of the alleged victim. The timeliness of such medical examination is particularly important. A medical examination should be undertaken regardless of the length of time since the torture, but if it is alleged to have happened within the past six weeks, such an examination should be arranged urgently before acute signs fade. The examination should include an assessment of the need for treatment of injuries and illnesses, psychological help, advice and follow-up (see chapter V for a description of the physical examination and forensic evaluation). A psychological appraisal of the alleged torture victim is always necessary and may be part of the physical examination, or where there are no physical signs, may be performed by itself (see chapter VI for a description of the psychological evaluation).

105. In formulating a clinical impression for the purpose of reporting physical and psychological evidence of torture, there are six important questions to ask:

(*a*) Are the physical and psychological findings consistent with the alleged report of torture?

(*b*) What physical conditions contribute to the clinical picture?

(*c*) Are the psychological findings expected or typical reactions to extreme stress within the cultural and social context of the individual?

(*d*) Given the fluctuating course of trauma-related mental disorders over time, what is the time frame in relation to the torture events? Where in the course of recovery is the individual?

(*e*) What other stressful factors are affecting the individual (e.g. ongoing persecution, forced migration, exile, loss of family and social role, etc.)? What impact do these issues have on the victim?

(*f*) Does the clinical picture suggest a false allegation of torture?

5. *Photography*

106. Colour photographs should be taken of the injuries of persons alleging that they have been tortured, of the premises where torture has allegedly occurred (interior and exterior) and of any other physical evidence found there. A measuring tape or some other means of showing scale on the photograph is essential. Photographs must be taken as soon as possible, even with a basic camera, because some physical signs fade rapidly and locations can be interfered with. Instantly developed photos may decay over time. More professional photos are preferred and should be taken as soon as the equipment becomes available. If possible, photographs should be taken using a 35-millimetre camera with an automatic date feature. The chain of custody of the film, negatives and prints must be fully documented.

D. Commission of inquiry

1. *Defining the scope of the inquiry*

107. States and organizations establishing commissions of inquiry need to define the scope of the inquiry by including terms of reference in their authorization. Defining the commission's terms of reference can greatly increase its success by giving legitimacy to the proceedings, assisting commission members in reaching a consensus on the scope of the inquiry and providing a measure by which the commission's final report can be judged. Recommendations for defining terms of reference are as follows:

(*a*) They should be neutrally framed so that they do not suggest a predetermined outcome. To be neutral, terms of reference must not limit investigations in areas that might uncover State responsibility for torture;

(*b*) They should state precisely which events and issues are to be investigated and addressed in the commission's final report;

(*c*) They should provide flexibility in the scope of inquiry to ensure that thorough investigation by the commission is not hampered by overly restrictive or overly broad terms of reference. The necessary flexibility may be accomplished, for example, by permitting the commission to amend its terms of reference as necessary. It is important, however, for the commission to keep the public informed of any amendments to its mandate.

2. *The power of the commission*

108. Principles should set out the powers of the commission in a general manner. The commission specifically needs the following:

(*a*) Authority to obtain all information necessary to the inquiry including the authority to compel testimony under legal sanction, to order the production of documents including State and medical records, and to protect witnesses, families of the victim and other sources;

(*b*) Authority to issue a public report;

(*c*) Authority to conduct on-site visits, including at the location where the torture is suspected to have occurred;

(*d*) Authority to receive evidence from witnesses and organizations located outside the country.

3. *Membership criteria*

109. Commission members should be chosen for their recognized impartiality, competence and independence as individuals as defined as follows:

(*a*) Impartiality. Commission members should not be closely associated with any individual, State entity, political party or other organization potentially implicated in the torture. They should not be too closely connected to an organization or group of which the victim is a member, as this may damage the commission's credibility. This should not, however, be an excuse for blanket exclusions from the commission, for instance, of members of large organizations of which the victim is also a member or of persons associated with organizations dedicated to the treatment and rehabilitation of torture victims;

(*b*) Competence. Commission members must be capable of evaluating and weighing evidence and exercising sound judgement. If possible, commissions of inquiry should include individuals with expertise in law, medicine and other appropriate specialized fields;

(*c*) Independence. Members of the commission should have a reputation in their community for honesty and fairness.

110. The objectivity of the investigation and the commission's findings may, among other things, depend on whether it has three or more members rather than one or two. A single commissioner should in general not conduct investigations into torture. A single, isolated commissioner will generally be limited in the depth of the investigation that he or she can conduct alone. In addition, a single commissioner will have to make controversial and important decisions without debate and will be particularly vulnerable to State and other outside pressure.

4. *The commission's staff*

111. Commissions of inquiry should have impartial, expert counsel. Where the commission is investigating allegations of State misconduct, it would be advisable to appoint counsel outside the Ministry of Justice. The chief counsel to the commission should be insulated from political influence, through civil service tenure or as a wholly independent member of the bar. The investigation will often require expert advisers. Technical expertise should be available to the commission in areas such as pathology, forensic science, psychiatry, psychology, gynaecology and paediatrics. To conduct a completely impartial and thorough investigation, the commission would almost always need its own investigators to pursue leads and develop evidence. The credibility of an inquiry would thus be significantly enhanced to the extent that the commission would be able to rely on its own investigators.

5. *Protection of witnesses*

112. The State shall protect complainants, witnesses, those conducting the investigation and their families from violence, threats of violence or any other form of intimidation (see section C.2 (*d*) above). If the commission concludes that there is a reasonable fear of persecution, harassment or harm to any witness or prospective witness, the commission may find it advisable to hear the evidence in camera, keep the identity of an informant or witness confidential, use only evidence that will not risk identifying the witness and take other appropriate measures.

6. *Proceedings*

113. It follows from general principles of criminal procedure that hearings should be conducted in public, unless in-camera proceedings are necessary to protect the safety of a witness. In-camera proceedings should be recorded and the sealed, unpublished record kept in a known location. Occasionally, complete secrecy may be required to encourage testimony, and the commission may want to hear witnesses privately, informally or without recording testimony.

7. *Notice of inquiry*

114. Wide notice of the establishment of a commission and the subject of the inquiry should be given. The notice should include an invitation to submit relevant information and written statements to the commission and instructions to persons willing to testify. Notice can be disseminated through newspapers, magazines, radio, television, leaflets and posters.

8. *Receipt of evidence*

115. Commissions of inquiry should have the power to compel testimony and produce documents, plus the authority to compel testimony from officials allegedly involved in torture. Practically, this authority may involve the power to impose fines or sentences if government officials or other individuals refuse to comply. Commissions

of inquiry should invite persons to testify or submit written statements as a first step in gathering evidence. Written statements may become an important source of evidence if their authors are afraid to testify, cannot travel to proceedings or are otherwise unavailable. Commissions of inquiry should review other proceedings that could provide relevant information.

9. *Rights of parties*

116. Those alleging that they have been tortured and their legal representatives should be informed of and have access to any hearing and all information relevant to the investigation and must be entitled to present evidence. This particular emphasis on the role of the survivor as a party to the proceedings reflects the especially important role his/her interests play in the conduct of the investigation. However, all other interested parties should also have an opportunity to be heard. The investigative body must be entitled to issue summonses to witnesses, including the officials allegedly involved, and to demand the production of evidence. All these witnesses should be permitted legal counsel if they are likely to be harmed by the inquiry, for example, when their testimony could expose them to criminal charges or civil liability. Witnesses may not be compelled to testify against themselves. There should be an opportunity for the effective questioning of witnesses by the commission. Parties to the inquiry should be allowed to submit written questions to the commission.

10. *Evaluation of evidence*

117. The commission must assess all information and evidence it receives to determine reliability and probity. The commission should evaluate oral testimony, taking into account the demeanour and overall credibility of the witness. The commission must be sensitive to social, cultural and gender issues that affect demeanour. Corroboration of evidence from several sources will increase the probative value of such evidence and the reliability of hearsay evidence. The reliability of hearsay evidence must be considered carefully before the commission accepts it as fact. Testimony not tested by cross-examination must also be viewed with caution. In-camera testimony preserved in a closed record or not recorded at all is often not subject to cross-examination and, therefore, may be given less weight.

11. *Report of the commission*

118. The commission should issue a public report within a reasonable period of time. Furthermore, when the commission is not unanimous in its findings, the minority commissioners should file a dissenting opinion. Commission of inquiry reports should contain, at a minimum, the following information:

(*a*) The scope of inquiry and terms of reference;

(*b*) The procedures and methods of evaluating evidence;

(*c*) A list of all witnesses, including age and gender, who have testified, except for those whose identities are withheld for protection or who have testified in camera, and exhibits received as evidence;

(*d*) The time and place of each sitting (this might be annexed to the report);

(*e*) The background of the inquiry, such as relevant social, political and economic conditions;

(*f*) The specific events that occurred and the evidence upon which such findings are based;

(*g*) The law upon which the commission relied;

(*h*) The commission's conclusions based on applicable law and findings of fact;

(*i*) Recommendations based on the findings of the commission.

119. The State should reply publicly to the commission's report and, where appropriate, indicate which steps it intends to take in response to the report.

CHAPTER IV

GENERAL CONSIDERATIONS FOR INTERVIEWS

120. When a person who has allegedly been tortured is interviewed, there are a number of issues and practical factors that have to be taken into consideration. These considerations apply to all persons carrying out interviews, whether they are lawyers, medical doctors, psychologists, psychiatrists, human rights monitors or members of any other profession. The following section takes up this "common ground" and attempts to put it into contexts that may be encountered when investigating torture and interviewing victims of torture.

A. Purpose of inquiry, examination and documentation

121. The broad purpose of the investigation is to establish the facts related to alleged incidents of torture (see chapter III, sect. D). Medical evaluations of torture may be useful evidence in legal contexts such as:

(a) Identifying the perpetrators responsible for torture and bringing them to justice;

(b) Support of political asylum applications;

(c) Establishing conditions under which false confessions may have been obtained by State officials;

(d) Establishing regional practices of torture. Medical evaluations may also be used to identify the therapeutic needs of survivors and as testimony in human rights investigations.

122. The purpose of the written or oral testimony of the physician is to provide expert opinion on the degree to which medical findings correlate with the patient's allegation of abuse and to communicate effectively the physician's medical findings and interpretations to the judiciary or other appropriate authorities. In addition, medical testimony often serves to educate the judiciary, other government officials and the local and international communities on the physical and psychological sequelae of torture. The examiner should be prepared to do the following:

(a) Assess possible injury and abuse, even in the absence of specific allegations by individuals, law enforcement or judicial officials;

(b) Document physical and psychological evidence of injury and abuse;

(c) Correlate the degree of consistency between examination findings and specific allegations of abuse by the patient;

(d) Correlate the degree of consistency between individual examination findings with the knowledge of torture methods used in a particular region and their common after-effects;

(e) Render expert interpretation of the findings of medical-legal evaluations and provide expert opinion regarding possible causes of abuse in asylum hearings, criminal trials and civil proceedings;

(f) Use information obtained in an appropriate manner to enhance fact-finding and further documentation of torture.

B. Procedural safeguards with respect to detainees

123. Forensic medical evaluation of detainees should be conducted in response to official written requests by public prosecutors or other appropriate officials. Requests for medical evaluations by law enforcement officials are to be considered invalid unless they are requested by written orders of a public prosecutor. Detainees themselves, their lawyers or relatives, however, have the right to request a medical evaluation to seek evidence of torture and ill-treatment. The detainee should be taken to the forensic medical examination by officials other than soldiers and police since torture and ill-treatment may have occurred in the custody of these officials and, therefore, that would place unacceptable coercive pressures on the detainee or the physician not to document torture or ill-treatment effectively. The officials who supervise the transportation of the detainee should be responsible to the public prosecutors and not to other law enforcement officials. The detainee's lawyer should be present during the request for examination and post-examination transport of the detainee. Detainees have the right to obtain a second or alternative medical evaluation by a qualified physician during and after the period of detention.

124. Each detainee must be examined in private. Police or other law enforcement officials should never be present in the examination room. This procedural safeguard may be precluded only when, in the opinion of the examining doctor, there is compelling evidence that the detainee poses a serious safety risk to health personnel. Under such circumstances, security personnel of the health facility, not the police or other law enforcement officials, should be available upon the medical examiner's request. In such cases, security personnel should still remain out of earshot (i.e. be only within visual contact) of the patient. Medical evaluation of detainees should be conducted at a location that the physician deems most

suitable. In some cases, it may be best to insist on evaluation at official medical facilities and not at the prison or jail. In other cases, prisoners may prefer to be examined in the relative safety of their cell, if they feel the medical premises may be under surveillance, for example. The best place will be dictated by many factors, but in all cases, investigators should ensure that prisoners are not forced into accepting a place with which they are not comfortable.

125.   The presence of police officers, soldiers, prison officers or other law enforcement officials in the examination room, for whatever reason, should be noted in the physician's official medical report. Their presence during the examination may be grounds for disregarding a negative medical report. The identity and titles of others who are present in the examination room during the medical evaluations should be indicated in the report. Medical-legal evaluations of detainees should include the use of a standardized medical report form (see annex IV for guidelines that may be used to develop standard medical report forms).

126.   The original, completed evaluation should be transmitted directly to the person requesting the report, generally the public prosecutor. When a detainee or a lawyer acting on his or her behalf requests a medical report, the report must be provided. Copies of all medical reports should be retained by the examining physician. A national medical association or a commission of inquiry may choose to audit medical reports to ensure that adequate procedural safeguards and documentation standards are adhered to, particularly by doctors employed by the State. Reports should be sent to such an organization, provided the issues of independence and confidentiality have been addressed. Under no circumstances should a copy of the medical report be transferred to law enforcement officials. It is mandatory that a detainee undergo a medical examination at the time of detention and an examination and evaluation upon release.[70] Access to a lawyer should be provided at the time of the medical examination. An outside presence during examination may be impossible in most prison situations. In such cases, it should be stipulated that prison doctors working with prisoners should respect medical ethics, and should be capable of carrying out their professional duties independently of any third-party influence. If the forensic medical examination supports allegations of torture, the detainee should not be returned to the place of detention, but rather should appear before the prosecutor or judge to determine the detainee's legal disposition.[71]

C.   Official visits to detention centres

127.   Visits to prisoners are not to be considered lightly. They can in some cases be notoriously difficult to carry out in an objective and professional way, particularly in countries where torture is still being practised.

One-off visits, without follow-up to ensure the safety of the interviewees after the visit, may be dangerous. In some cases, one visit without a repeat visit may be worse than no visit at all. Well-meaning investigators may fall into the trap of visiting a prison or police station, without knowing exactly what they are doing. They may obtain an incomplete or false picture of reality. They may inadvertently place prisoners that they may never visit again in danger. They may give an alibi to the perpetrators of torture, who may use the fact that outsiders visited their prison and saw nothing.

128.   Visits should best be left to investigators who can carry them out and follow them up in a professional way and who have certain weathered procedural safeguards for their work. The notion that some evidence is better than no evidence is not valid when working with prisoners who might be put in danger by giving testimony. Visits to detention facilities by well-meaning people representing official and non-governmental institutions can be difficult and, worse, can be counter-productive. In the case in point here, a distinction should be made between a bona fide visit necessary for the inquiry, which is not in question, and a non-essential visit that goes beyond that, which when made by non-specialists could cause more harm than good in a country that practises torture. Independent commissions constituted by jurists and physicians should be given ensured periodic access to visit places of detention and prisons.

129.   Interviews with people who are still in custody, and possibly even in the hands of the perpetrators of torture will obviously be very different from interviews in the privacy and security of an outside, safe medical facility. The importance of obtaining the person's trust in such situations cannot be stressed enough. However, it is even more important not, even unwittingly, to betray that trust. All precautions should be taken to ensure that detainees do not place themselves in danger. Detainees who have been tortured should be asked whether the information can be used and in what way. They may be too afraid to allow use of their names, fearing reprisals for example. Investigators, clinicians and interpreters are bound to respect that which has been promised to the detainee.

130.   A clear dilemma may arise if, for example, it is evident that a large number of prisoners have been tortured in a given place, but they all refuse to allow investigators to use their stories because of fear. The options are either betraying the prisoners' trust in the effort to stop torture or respecting trust and going away without saying anything; a useful way has to be found out of this dilemma. When confronted with a number of prisoners with clear signs on their bodies of whippings, beatings, lacerations caused by canings, etc., but who all refuse mention of their cases out of fear of reprisal, it is useful to organize a "health inspection" of the whole ward in full view in the courtyard. In that way, the visiting medical investigator walking through the ranks and directly observing the very visible signs of torture on the backs of the prisoners is able to make a report on what he has seen and will not have to say that prisoners complained about torture. This first step ensures the prisoners' trust for future follow-up visits.

---

[70] See the United Nations Standard Minimum Rules for the Treatment of Prisoners (chap. I, sect. B).

[71] "Health care for prisoners: implications of Kalk's refusal", *The Lancet,* vol. 337 (1991), pp. 647-648.

131. Other more subtle forms of torture, psychological or sexual, for example, clearly cannot be dealt with in the same way. In these cases, it may be necessary for investigators to refrain from comment for one or several visits until the circumstances allow or encourage detainees to be less afraid and to authorize the use of their stories. The physician and interpreter should provide their names and explain their role in conducting the evaluation. Documentation of medical evidence of torture requires specific knowledge by licensed health practitioners. Knowledge of torture and its physical and psychological consequences can be gained through publications, training courses, professional conferences and experience. In addition, knowledge about regional practices of torture and ill-treatment is important because such information may corroborate an individual's accounts of these. Experience in interviewing and examining individuals for physical and psychological evidence of torture and in documenting findings should be acquired under the supervision of experienced clinicians.

132. Those still in custody may sometimes be too trusting in situations where the interviewer simply cannot guarantee that there will be no reprisals, if a repeat visit has not been negotiated and fully accepted by the authorities or if the person's identity has not been recorded so as to ensure follow-up, for example. Every precaution should be taken to be sure that prisoners do not place themselves at risk unnecessarily, naively trusting an outsider to protect them.

133. Ideally, when visits are made to people still in custody the interpreters should be outsiders and not recruited locally. This is mainly to avoid them or their families being put under pressure from inquisitive authorities wanting to know what information was given to the investigators. The issue may be more complex when the detainees are from a different ethnic group than their jailers. Should the local interpreter be from the same ethnic group as the prisoner, so as to gain his/her trust, but at the same time arousing the mistrust of the authorities who would possibly attempt to intimidate the interpreter? Furthermore, the interpreter may be reluctant to work in a hostile environment, which would potentially place him or her at risk. Or should the interpreter come from the same ethnic group as the captors, thereby gaining trust, but losing that of the prisoner, while still leaving the interpreter vulnerable to intimidation by the authorities? The answer is obviously and ideally neither of the above. Interpreters should be from outside the region and seen by all to be as independent as the investigators.

134. A person interviewed at 8 p.m. deserves as much attention as one seen at 8 a.m. Investigators should arrange to have enough time and not overwork themselves. It is unfair to the 8 p.m. person (who in addition has been waiting all day to tell his or her story) to be cut short because of the time. Similarly, the nineteenth story about *falanga* deserves as much attention as the first. Prisoners who do not often see outsiders may never have had a chance to talk about their torture. It is an erroneous assumption to think that prisoners talk constantly among themselves about torture. Prisoners who have nothing new to offer the investigation deserve as much time as the other prisoners.

D. Techniques of questioning

135. Several basic rules must be respected (see chapter III, sect. C.2 (*g*)). Information is certainly important, but the person being interviewed is even more so, and listening is more important than asking questions. If only questions are asked, all that are obtained are answers. To the detainee, it may be more important to talk about family than to talk about torture. This should be duly considered, and time should be allowed for some discussion of personal matters. Torture, particularly sexual torture, is a very intimate subject and may not come up before a follow-up visit or even later. Individuals should not be forced to talk about any form of torture if they feel uncomfortable about it.

E. Documenting the background

1. *Psychosocial history and pre-arrest*

136. If an alleged torture victim is no longer in custody, the examiner should inquire into the person's daily life, relations with friends and family, work or school, occupation, interests, future plans and use of alcohol and drugs. Information should also be elicited regarding the person's post-detention psychosocial history. When an individual is still in custody, a more limited psychosocial history regarding occupation and literacy is sufficient. Inquire about prescription medication being taken by the patient; this is particularly important because such medications may be denied to a person in custody, with significant adverse health consequences. Inquiries into political activities, beliefs and opinions are relevant insofar as they help to explain why a person was detained or tortured, but such inquiries are best made indirectly by asking the person which accusations were made or why they think they were detained and tortured.

2. *Summary of detention and abuse*

137. Before obtaining a detailed account of events, elicit summary information, including dates, places, duration of detention, frequency and duration of torture sessions. A summary will help to make effective use of time. In some cases in which survivors have been tortured on multiple occasions, they may be able to recall what happened to them, but often they cannot recall exactly where and when each event occurred. In such circumstances, it may be advisable to elicit the historical account according to methods of abuse rather than relating a series of events during specific arrests. Similarly, in writing up the story it may often be useful to have "what happened where" documented as much as possible. Holding places are operated by different security, police or armed forces, and what happened in different places may be useful for a full picture of the torture system. Obtaining a map of where the torture occurred may be useful in piecing together the stories of different people. This will often prove very useful for the overall investigation.

3. *Circumstances of detention*

138. Consider the following questions: what time was it? Where were you? What were you doing? Who was there? Describe the appearance of those who detained you. Were they military or civilian, in uniform or in street clothes? What type of weapons were they carrying? What was said? Any witnesses? Was this a formal arrest, administrative detention or disappearance? Was violence used, threats spoken? Was there any interaction with family members? Note the use of restraints or blindfold, means of transportation, destination and names of officials, if known.

4. *Place and conditions of detention*

139. Include access to and descriptions of food and drink, toilet facilities, lighting, temperature and ventilation. Also, document any contact with family, lawyers or health professionals, conditions of overcrowding or solitary confinement, dimensions of the detention place and whether there are other people who can corroborate the detention. Consider the following questions: what happened first? Where were you taken? Was there an identification process (personal information recorded, fingerprints, photographs)? Were you asked to sign anything? Describe the conditions of the cell or room (note size, others present, light, ventilation, temperature, presence of insects, rodents, bedding and access to food, water and toilet). What did you hear, see and smell? Did you have any contact with people outside or access to medical care? What was the physical layout of the place where you were detained?

5. *Methods of torture and ill-treatment*

140. In obtaining background information on torture and ill-treatment, caution should be used about suggesting forms of abuse to which a person may have been subjected. This may help separate potential embellishment from valid experiences. However, eliciting negative responses to questions about various forms of torture may also help establish the credibility of the person. Questions should be designed to elicit a coherent narrative account. Consider the following questions. Where did the abuse take place, when and for how long? Were you blindfolded? Before discussing forms of abuse, note who was present (give names, positions). Describe the room or place. Which objects did you observe? If possible, describe each instrument of torture in detail; for electrical torture, the current, device, number and shape of electrodes. Ask about clothing, disrobing and change of clothing. Record quotations of what was said during interrogation, insults hurled at the victim, etc. What was said among the perpetrators?

141. For each form of abuse, note: body position, restraint, nature of contact, including duration, frequency, anatomical location and the area of the body affected. Was there any bleeding, head trauma or loss of consciousness? Was the loss of consciousness due to head trauma, asphyxiation or pain? The investigator should also ask about how the person was at the end of the "session". Could he or she walk? Did he or she have to be helped or carried back to the cell? Could he or she get up the next day? How long did the feet stay swollen? All this gives a certain completeness to the description, which a checklist of methods does not. The history should include the date of positional torture, how many times and for how many days the torture lasted, the period of each episode, the style of the suspension (reverse-linear, being covered by thick cloth-blanket or being tied directly with a rope, putting weight on the legs or pulling down) or position. In cases of suspension torture, ask which sort of material was used (rope, wire and cloth leave different marks, if any, on the skin after suspension). The examiner must remember that statements on the length of the torture session by the torture survivor are subjective and may not be correct, since disorientation of time and place during torture is a generally observed finding. Was the person sexually assaulted in any manner? Elicit what was said during the torture. For example, during electric shock torture to the genitals, perpetrators often tell their torture victims that they will no longer have normal sexual relations or something similar. For a detailed discussion of the assessment of an allegation of sexual torture, including rape, see chapter V, sect. D.8.

F. Assessment of the background

142. Torture survivors may have difficulty recounting the specific details of the torture for several important reasons, including:

(*a*) Factors during torture itself, such as blindfolding, drugging, lapses of consciousness, etc.;

(*b*) Fear of placing themselves or others at risk;

(*c*) A lack of trust in the examining clinician or interpreter;

(*d*) The psychological impact of torture and trauma, such as high emotional arousal and impaired memory, secondary to trauma-related mental illnesses, such as depression and post-traumatic stress disorder (PTSD);

(*e*) Neuropsychiatric memory impairment from beatings to the head, suffocation, near drowning or starvation;

(*f*) Protective coping mechanisms, such as denial and avoidance;

(*g*) Culturally prescribed sanctions that allow traumatic experiences to be revealed only in highly confidential settings.[72]

143. Inconsistencies in a person's story may arise from any or all of these factors. If possible, the investigator should ask for further clarification. When this is not possible, the investigator should look for other evidence that supports or refutes the story. A network of consistent supporting details can corroborate and clarify the person's story. Although the individual may not be able to provide the details desired by the investigator, such as dates, times, frequencies and exact identities of perpetrators, a broad outline of the traumatic events and torture will emerge and stand up over time.

---

[72] R. F. Mollica and Y. Caspi-Yavin, "Overview: the assessment and diagnosis of torture events and symptoms", in *Torture and Its Consequences: Current Treatment Approaches*, M. Başoğlu, ed. (Cambridge, Cambridge University Press, 1992), pp. 38-55.

G. Review of torture methods

144.   After eliciting a detailed narrative account of events, it is advisable to review other possible torture methods. It is essential to learn about regional practices of torture and modify local guidelines accordingly. Questioning about specific forms of torture is helpful when:

(*a*) Psychological symptoms cloud recollections;

(*b*) The trauma was associated with impaired sensory capabilities;

(*c*) There is a case of possible organic brain damage;

(*d*) There are mitigating educational and cultural factors.

145.   The distinction between physical and psychological methods is artificial. For example, sexual torture generally causes both physical and psychological symptoms, even when there has been no physical assault. The following list of torture methods is given to show some of the categories of possible abuse. It is not meant to be used by investigators as a checklist or as a model for listing torture methods in a report. A method-listing approach may be counter-productive, as the entire clinical picture produced by torture is much more than the simple sum of lesions produced by methods on a list. Indeed, experience has shown that when confronted with such a "package-deal" approach to torture, perpetrators often focus on one of the methods and argue about whether that particular method is a form of torture. Torture methods to consider include, but are not limited to:

(*a*) Blunt trauma, such as a punch, kick, slap, whipping, a beating with wires or truncheons or falling down;

(*b*) Positional torture, using suspension, stretching limbs apart, prolonged constraint of movement, forced positioning;

(*c*) Burns with cigarettes, heated instruments, scalding liquid or a caustic substance;

(*d*) Electric shocks;

(*e*) Asphyxiation, such as wet and dry methods, drowning, smothering, choking or use of chemicals;

(*f*) Crush injuries, such as smashing fingers or using a heavy roller to injure the thighs or back;

(*g*) Penetrating injuries, such as stab and gunshot wounds, wires under nails;

(*h*) Chemical exposure to salt, chilli pepper, gasoline, etc. (in wounds or body cavities);

(*i*) Sexual violence to genitals, molestation, instrumentation, rape;

(*j*) Crush injury or traumatic removal of digits and limbs;

(*k*) Medical amputation of digits or limbs, surgical removal of organs;

(*l*) Pharmacological torture using toxic doses of sedatives, neuroleptics, paralytics, etc.;

(*m*) Conditions of detention, such as a small or over-crowded cell, solitary confinement, unhygienic conditions, no access to toilet facilities, irregular or contaminated food and water, exposure to extremes of temperature, denial of privacy and forced nakedness;

(*n*) Deprivation of normal sensory stimulation, such as sound, light, sense of time, isolation, manipulation of brightness of the cell, abuse of physiological needs, restriction of sleep, food, water, toilet facilities, bathing, motor activities, medical care, social contacts, isolation within prison, loss of contact with the outside world (victims are often kept in isolation in order to prevent bonding and mutual identification and to encourage traumatic bonding with the torturer);

(*o*) Humiliation, such as verbal abuse, performance of humiliating acts;

(*p*) Threats of death, harm to family, further torture, imprisonment, mock executions;

(*q*) Threats of attack by animals, such as dogs, cats, rats or scorpions;

(*r*) Psychological techniques to break down the individual, including forced betrayals, accentuating feelings of helplessness, exposure to ambiguous situations or contradictory messages;

(*s*) Violation of taboos;

(*t*) Behavioural coercion, such as forced engagement in practices against the religion of the victim (e.g. forcing Muslims to eat pork), forced harm to others through torture or other abuses, forced destruction of property, forced betrayal of someone placing them at risk of harm;

(*u*) Forcing the victim to witness torture or atrocities being inflicted on others.

H.   Risk of re-traumatization of the interviewee

146.   Taking into consideration that lesions of different types and levels may occur according to the methods of torture practised, the data acquired subsequent to a comprehensive medical history and physical examination should be assessed together with appropriate laboratory and radiological examinations. Providing information and making explanations for each process to be applied during the medical examination and ensuring detailed awareness about the laboratory methods play a significant role (see chapter VI, sect. B.2 (*a*)).

147.   The presence of psychological sequelae in torture survivors, particularly the various manifestations of PTSD, may cause the torture survivor to fear experiencing a re-enactment of his or her torture experience during the interview, physical examination or laboratory test. Explaining to the torture survivor what he or she should expect prior to the medical examination is an important component of the process. Those who survive torture and remain in their country may experience intense fear and suspicion about being re-arrested, and they are often forced to go underground to avoid being arrested again. Those who are exiled or refugees may leave behind their native language, culture, family, friends, work and everything that is familiar to them.

148.   The torture survivor's personal reactions to the interviewer (and the interpreter, in cases where one is used) can have an effect on the interview process and, in

turn, the outcome of the investigation. Likewise, the personal reactions of the investigator towards the person can also affect the process of the interview and the outcome of the investigation. It is important to examine the barriers to effective communication and the understanding that these personal reactions might impose on an investigation. The investigator should maintain an ongoing examination of the interview and investigation process through consultation and discussion with colleagues familiar with the field of psychological assessment and treatment of torture survivors. This type of peer supervision can be an effective means of monitoring the interview and investigation process for biases and barriers to effective communication and for obtaining accurate information (see chapter VI, sect. C.2).

149.   Despite all precautions, physical and psychological examinations by their very nature may re-traumatize the patient by provoking or exacerbating symptoms of post-traumatic stress by reviving painful effects and memories (see chapter VI, sect. B.2). Questions about psychological distress and, especially, about sexual matters are considered taboo in most traditional societies, and the asking of such questions is regarded as irreverent or insulting. If sexual torture was part of the violations incurred, the claimant may feel irredeemably stigmatized and tainted in his or her moral, religious, social or psychological integrity. The expression of a respectful awareness of these conditions, as well as the clarification of confidentiality and its limits, are, therefore, of paramount importance for a well-conducted interview. A subjective assessment has to be made by the evaluator about the extent to which pressing for details is necessary for the effectiveness of the report in court, especially if the claimant demonstrates obvious signs of distress in the interview.

I.   Use of interpreters

150.   For many purposes, it is necessary to use an interpreter to allow the interviewer to understand what is being said. Although the interviewer and the interviewee may share a little of a common language, the information being sought is often too important to risk the errors that arise from an incomplete understanding of one another. Interpreters must be advised that what they hear and interpret in interviews is strictly confidential. It is the interpreters who get all the information, first-hand and uncensored. Individuals must be given assurances that neither the investigator nor the interpreter will misuse information in any way (see chapter VI, sect. C.2).

151.   When the interpreter is not a professional, there is always the risk of the investigator losing control of the interview. Individuals may be carried away talking to the person who speaks their language, and the interview may divert from the issues at hand. There is also a risk that an interpreter with a bias might lead the interviewee on or distort the replies. Loss of information, sometimes relevant, sometimes not, is inevitable when working through interpretation. In extreme cases, it may even be necessary for investigators to refrain from taking notes during interviews and carry out interviews in several short sessions,

so as to have time to write down the main points of what has been said between sessions.

152.   Investigators should remember to talk to the person and to maintain eye contact, even if he or she has a natural tendency to speak to the interpreter. It helps to use the second person when speaking through the interpreter, for example "what did you do next", rather than the third person "ask him what happened next". All too often, investigators write their notes during the time when the interpreter is either translating the question or the interviewee answering it. Some investigators do not appear to be listening, as the interview is going on in a language they do not understand. This should not be the case, as it is essential for investigators to observe not just the words but also the body language, facial expressions, tone of voice and gestures of the interviewee if they are to obtain a full picture. Investigators should familiarize themselves with torture-related words in the person's language so as to show that they know about the issue. Reacting, rather than showing a blank face, when hearing a torture-related word such as *submarino* or *darmashakra* will add to the investigator's credibility.

153.   When visiting prisoners, it is best never to use local interpreters if there is a possibility of their being considered untrustworthy by those interviewed. It may also be unfair for the local interpreters, who may be "debriefed" by the local authorities after a visit, or otherwise put under pressure, to be involved with political prisoners. It is best to use independent interpreters, clearly seen as coming from elsewhere. The next best thing to speaking the local language fluently is to work with a trained interpreter with experience, who is sensitive to the issue of torture and to the local culture. As a rule, co-detainees should not be used for interpretation, unless it is obvious that the interviewee has chosen someone he or she trusts. In the case of people who are not in detention, many of these same rules also apply, but it may be easier to bring in someone (a local person) from the outside, which is rarely possible in prison situations.

J.   Gender issues

154.   Ideally, an investigation team should contain specialists of both genders, permitting the person who says that they have been tortured to choose the gender of the investigator and, where necessary, the interpreter. This is particularly important when a woman has been detained in a situation where rape is known to happen, even if she has not, so far, complained of it. Even if no sexual assault takes place, most torture has sexual aspects (see chapter V, sect. D.8). The re-traumatization can often be worse if she feels she has to describe what happened to a person who is physically similar to her torturers, who will inevitably have been mostly or entirely men. In some cultures, it would be impossible for a male investigator to question a female victim, and this must be respected. However, in most cultures, if there is only a male physician available, many women would prefer to talk to him rather than a female of another profession in order to gain the medical information and advice that she wants. In such a case, it is essential that the interpreter, if used, be female. Some interviewees may also prefer that the interpreter be from

outside their immediate locality, both because of the danger of being reminded of their torture and because of the perceived threat to their confidentiality (see chapter IV, sect. I). If no interpreter is necessary, then a female member of the investigating team should be present as a chaperone throughout at least the physical examination and, if the patient wishes, throughout the entire interview.

155.   When the victim is male and has been sexually abused, the situation is more complex because he too will have been sexually abused mostly or entirely by men. Some men would, therefore, prefer to describe their experiences to women because their fear of other men is so great, while others would not want to discuss such personal matters in front of a woman.

K.   Indications for referral

156.   Wherever possible, examinations to document torture for medical-legal reasons should be combined with an assessment for other needs, whether referral to specialist physicians, psychologists, physiotherapists or those who can offer social advice and support. Investigators should be aware of local rehabilitation and support services. The clinician should not hesitate to insist on any consultation and examination that he or she considers necessary in a medical evaluation. In the course of documenting medical evidence of torture and ill-treatment, physicians are not absolved of their ethical obligations. Those who appear to be in need of further medical or psychological care should be referred to the appropriate services.

L.   Interpretation of findings and conclusions

157.   Physical manifestations of torture may vary according to the intensity, frequency and duration of abuse, the torture survivor's ability to protect him or herself and the physical condition of the detainee prior to the torture. Other forms of torture may not produce physical findings, but may be associated with other conditions. For example, beatings to the head that result in loss of consciousness can cause post-traumatic epilepsy or organic brain dysfunction. Also, poor diet and hygiene in detention can cause vitamin deficiency syndromes.

158.   Certain forms of torture are strongly associated with particular sequelae. For example, beatings to the head that result in loss of consciousness are particularly important to the clinical diagnosis of organic brain dysfunction. Trauma to the genitals is often associated with subsequent sexual dysfunction.

159.   It is important to realize that torturers may attempt to conceal their acts. To avoid physical evidence of beating, torture is often performed with wide, blunt objects, and torture victims are sometimes covered with a rug, or shoes in the case of *falanga*, to distribute the force of individual blows. Stretching, crushing injuries and asphyxiation are also forms of torture with the intention of producing maximal pain and suffering with minimal evidence. For the same reason, wet towels are used with electric shocks.

160.   The report must list the qualifications and experience of the investigator. Where possible, the name of the witness or patient should be given. If this puts the person at significant risk, an identifier can be used that allows the investigating team to relate the person to the record, but that will not allow anyone else to identify the individual. The report must indicate who else was in the room at the time of the interview or any part of it. It should detail the relevant history, avoiding hearsay and, where appropriate, report the findings. It must be signed, dated and include any necessary declaration required by the jurisdiction for which it is written (see annex IV).

Chapter V

PHYSICAL EVIDENCE OF TORTURE

161. Witness and survivor testimony are necessary components in the documentation of torture. To the extent that physical evidence of torture exists, it provides important confirmatory evidence that a person has been tortured. However, the absence of such physical evidence should not be construed to suggest that torture did not occur, since such acts of violence against persons frequently leave no marks or permanent scars.

162. A medical evaluation for legal purposes should be conducted with objectivity and impartiality. The evaluation should be based on the physician's clinical expertise and professional experience. The ethical obligation of beneficence demands uncompromising accuracy and impartiality in order to establish and maintain professional credibility. When possible, clinicians who conduct evaluations of detainees should have specific essential training in forensic documentation of torture and other forms of physical and psychological abuse. They should have knowledge of prison conditions and torture methods used in the particular region where the patient was imprisoned and the common after-effects of torture. The medical report should be factual and carefully worded. Jargon should be avoided. All medical terminology should be defined so that it is understandable to lay persons. The physician should not assume that the official requesting a medical-legal evaluation has related all the material facts. It is the physician's responsibility to discover and report upon any material findings that he or she considers relevant, even if they may be considered irrelevant or adverse to the case of the party requesting the medical examination. Findings that are consistent with torture or other forms of ill-treatment must not be excluded from a medical-legal report under any circumstance.

A. Interview structure

163. These comments apply especially to interviews conducted with persons no longer in custody. The location of the interview and examination should be as safe and comfortable as possible. Sufficient time should be allotted to conduct a detailed interview and examination. A two-to-four-hour interview may be insufficient to conduct an evaluation for physical or psychological evidence of torture. Furthermore, at any given time of an evaluation, situation-specific variables, such as the dynamics of the interview, a patient's feelings of powerlessness in the face of having his/her intimacy intruded upon, fear of future persecution, shame about events and survivor guilt may simulate the circumstances of a torture experience. This may increase the patient's anxiety and resistance to disclose relevant information. A second, and possibly a third,

interview may have to be scheduled to complete the evaluation.

164. Trust is an essential component of eliciting an accurate account of abuse. Earning the trust of someone who has experienced torture or other forms of abuse requires active listening, meticulous communication, courtesy and genuine empathy and honesty. Physicians must have the capacity to create a climate of trust in which disclosure of crucial, though perhaps very painful or shameful, facts can occur. It is important to be aware that those facts are sometimes intimate secrets that the person may reveal at that moment for the first time. In addition to providing a comfortable setting, adequate time for the interviews, refreshments and access to toilet facilities, the clinician should explain what the patient can expect in the evaluation. The clinician should be mindful of the tone, phrasing and sequencing of questions (sensitive questions should be asked only after some degree of rapport has been developed) and should acknowledge the patient's ability to take a break if needed or to choose not to respond to any question.

165. Physicians and interpreters have a duty to maintain confidentiality of information and to disclose information only with the patient's consent (see chapter III, sect. C). Each person should be examined individually with privacy. He or she should be informed of any limits on the confidentiality of the evaluation that may be imposed by State or judicial authorities. The purpose of the interview needs to be made clear to the person. Physicians must ensure that informed consent is based on adequate disclosure and understanding of the potential benefits and adverse consequences of a medical evaluation and that consent is given voluntarily without coercion by others, particularly law enforcement or judicial authorities. The person has the right to refuse the evaluation. In such circumstances, the clinician should document the reason for refusal of an evaluation. Furthermore, if the person is a detainee, the report should be signed by his or her lawyer and another health official.

166. Patients may fear that information revealed in the context of an evaluation may not be safely kept from being accessed by persecuting governments. Fear and mistrust may be particularly strong in cases where physicians or other health workers were participants in the torture. In many circumstances, the evaluator will be a member of the majority culture and ethnicity, whereas the patient, in the situation and location of the interview, is likely to belong to a minority group or culture. This dynamic of inequality may reinforce the perceived and real imbalance of power and may increase the potential

sense of fear, mistrust and forced submission in the patient.

167. Empathy and human contact may be the most important thing that people still in custody receive from the investigator. The investigation itself may contribute nothing of specific benefit to the person being interviewed, as in most cases their torture will be over. The meagre consolation of knowing that the information may serve a future purpose will however be greatly enhanced if the investigator shows appropriate empathy. While this may seem self-evident, all too often investigators in prison visits are so concerned about obtaining information that they fail to empathize with the prisoner being interviewed.

B. Medical history

168. Obtain a complete medical history, including information about prior medical, surgical or psychiatric problems. Be sure to document any history of injuries before the period of detention and any possible after-effects. Avoid leading questions. Structure inquiries to elicit an open-ended, chronological account of the events experienced during detention.

169. Specific historical information may be useful in correlating regional practices of torture with individual allegations of abuse. Examples of useful information include descriptions of torture devices, body positions, methods of restraint, descriptions of acute or chronic wounds and disabilities and identifying information about perpetrators and places of detention. While it is essential to obtain accurate information regarding a torture survivor's experiences, open-ended interviewing methods require that patients should disclose these experiences in their own words using free recall. An individual who has survived torture may have trouble expressing in words his or her experiences and symptoms. In some cases, it may be helpful to use these trauma event and symptom checklists or questionnaires. If the interviewer believes it may be helpful to use these, there are numerous questionnaires available; however, none are specific to torture victims. All complaints made by a torture survivor are significant. Although there may be no correlation with the physical findings, they should be reported. Acute and chronic symptoms and disabilities associated with specific forms of abuse and the subsequent healing processes should be documented.

1. *Acute symptoms*

170. The individual should be asked to describe any injuries that may have resulted from the specific methods of alleged abuse. These can be, for example, bleeding, bruising, swelling, open wounds, lacerations, fractures, dislocations, joint stress, haemoptysis, pneumothorax, tympanic membrane perforation, genito-urinary system injuries, burns (colour, bulla or necrosis according to the degree of burn), electrical injuries (size and number of lesions, their colour and surface characteristics), chemical injuries (colour, signs of necrosis), pain, numbness, constipation and vomiting. The intensity, frequency and duration of each symptom should be noted. The development of any subsequent skin lesions should be described indi-

cating whether or not they left scars. Ask about health on release; was he or she able to walk or confined to bed? If confined, for how long? How long did wounds take to heal? Were they infected? What treatment was received? Was it a physician or a traditional healer? Be aware that the detainee's ability to make such observations may have been compromised by the torture itself or its after-effects and should be documented.

2. *Chronic symptoms*

171. Elicit information on physical ailments that the individual believes were associated with torture or ill-treatment. Note the severity, frequency and duration of each symptom and any associated disability or need for medical or psychological care. Even if the after-effects of acute lesions cannot be seen months or years later, some physical findings may still remain, such as electrical current or thermal burn scars, skeletal deformities, incorrect healing of fractures, dental injuries, loss of hair and myofibrosis. Common somatic complaints include headache, back pain, gastrointestinal symptoms, sexual dysfunction and muscle pain. Common psychological symptoms include depressive affect, anxiety, insomnia, nightmares, flashbacks and memory difficulties (see chapter VI, sect. B.2).

3. *Summary of an interview*

172. Torture victims may have injuries that are substantially different from other forms of trauma. Although acute lesions may be characteristic of the alleged injuries, most lesions heal within about six weeks of torture, leaving no scars or, at the most, non-specific scars. This is often the case when torturers use techniques that prevent or limit detectable signs of injury. Under such circumstances, the physical examination may be within normal limits, but this in no way negates allegations of torture. A detailed account of the patient's observations of acute lesions and the subsequent healing process often represents an important source of evidence in corroborating specific allegations of torture or ill-treatment.

C. The physical examination

173. Subsequent to the acquisition of background information and after the patient's informed consent has been obtained, a complete physical examination by a qualified physician should be performed. Whenever possible, the patient should be able to choose the gender of the physician and, where used, of the interpreter. If the doctor is not of the same gender as the patient, a chaperone who is should be used unless the patient objects. The patient must understand that he or she is in control and has the right to limit the examination or to stop it at any time (see chapter IV, sect. J).

174. In this section, there are many references to specialist referral and further investigations. Unless the patient is in detention, it is important for physicians to have access to physical and psychological treatment facilities, so that any identified need can be followed up. In many situations, certain diagnostic test techniques will

not be available, and their absence must not invalidate the report (see annex II for further details of possible diagnostic tests).

175. In cases of alleged recent torture and when the clothes worn during torture are still being worn by the torture survivor, they should be taken for examination without having been washed, and a fresh set of clothes should be provided. Wherever possible, the examination room should be equipped with sufficient light and medical equipment for the examination. Any deficiencies should be noted in the report. The examiner should note all pertinent positive and negative findings, using body diagrams to record the location and nature of all injuries (see annex III). Some forms of torture such as electrical shock or blunt trauma may be initially undetectable, but may be detected during a follow-up examination. Although it will rarely be possible to record photographically lesions of prisoners in custody of their torturers, photography should be a routine part of examinations. If a camera is available, it is always better to take poor quality photographs than to have none. They should be followed up with professional photographs as soon as possible (see chapter III, sect. C.5).

1. Skin

176. The examination should include the entire body surface in order to detect signs of generalized skin disease including signs of vitamin A, B and C deficiency, pre-torture lesions or lesions inflicted by torture, such as abrasions, contusions, lacerations, puncture wounds, burns from cigarettes or heated instruments, electrical injuries, alopecia and nail removal. Torture lesions should be described by their localization, symmetry, shape, size, colour and surface (e.g. scaly, crusty, ulcerating) as well as their demarcation and level in relation to the surrounding skin. Photography is essential whenever possible. Ultimately, the examiner must offer an opinion as to the origin of the lesions: inflicted or self-inflicted, accidental or the result of a disease process.[73, 74]

2. Face

177. Facial tissues should be palpated for evidence of fracture, crepitation, swelling or pain. The motor and sensory components, including smell and taste of all cranial nerves, should be examined. Computerized tomography (CT), rather than routine radiography, is the best modality to diagnose and characterize facial fractures, determine alignment and diagnose associated soft tissue injuries and complications. Intracranial and cervical spinal injuries are often associated with facial trauma.

---

[73] O. V. Rasmussen, "Medical aspects of torture", *Danish Medical Bulletin*, vol. 37, supplement No. 1 (1990), pp. 1-88.

[74] R. Bunting, "Clinical examinations in the police context", *Clinical Forensic Medicine*, W. D. S. McLay, ed. (London, Greenwich Medical Media, 1996), pp. 59-73.

(a) Eyes

178. There are many forms of trauma to the eyes, including conjunctival haemorrhage, lens dislocation, subhyeloid haemorrhage, retrobulbar haemorrhage, retinal haemorrhage and visual field loss. Given the serious consequences of lack of treatment or improper treatment, ophthalmologic consultation should be obtained whenever there is a suspicion of ocular trauma or disease. CT is the best modality to diagnose orbital fractures and soft tissue injuries to the bulbar and retrobulbar contents. Nuclear magnetic resonance imaging (MRI) may be an adjunct for identifying soft tissue injury. High resolution ultrasound is an alternative method for evaluation of trauma to the eye globe.

(b) Ears

179. Trauma to the ears, especially rupture of the tympanic membrane, is a frequent consequence of harsh beatings. The ear canals and tympanic membranes should be examined with an otoscope and injuries described. A common form of torture, known in Latin America as *telefono*, is a hard slap of the palm to one or both ears, rapidly increasing pressure in the ear canal, thus rupturing the drum. Prompt examination is necessary to detect tympanic membrane ruptures less than 2 millimetres in diameter, which may heal within 10 days. Fluid may be observed in the middle or external ear. If otorrhea is confirmed by laboratory analysis, MRI or CT should be performed to determine the fracture site. The presence of hearing loss should be investigated, using simple screening methods. If necessary, audiometric tests should be conducted by a qualified audiometric technician. The radiographic examination of fractures of the temporal bone or disruption of the ossicular chain is best determined by CT, then hypocycloidal tomography and, lastly, linear tomography.

(c) Nose

180. The nose should be evaluated for alignment, crepitation and deviation of the nasal septum. For simple nasal fractures, standard nasal radiographs should be sufficient. For complex nasal fractures and when the cartilaginous septum is displaced, CT should be performed. If rhinorrhea is present, CT or MRI is recommended.

(d) Jaw, oropharynx and neck

181. Mandibular fractures or dislocations may result from beatings. Temporomandibular joint syndrome is a frequent consequence of beatings about the lower face and jaw. The patient should be examined for evidence of crepitation of the hyoid bone or laryngeal cartilage resulting from blows to the neck. Findings concerning the oropharynx should be noted in detail, including lesions consistent with burns from electrical shock or other trauma. Gingival haemorrhage and the condition of the gums should also be noted.

(e) Oral cavity and teeth

182. Examination by a dentist should be considered a component of periodic health examination in detention. This examination is often neglected, but it is an important

component of the physical examination. Dental care may be purposefully withheld to allow caries, gingivitis or tooth abscesses to worsen. A careful dental history should be taken, and, if dental records exist, they should be requested. Tooth avulsions, fractures of the teeth, dislocated fillings and broken prostheses may result from direct trauma or electric shock torture. Dental caries and gingivitis should be noted. Poor quality dentition may be due to conditions in detention or may have preceded the detention. The oral cavity must be carefully examined. During application of an electric current, the tongue, gums or lips may be bitten. Lesions might be produced by forcing objects or materials into the mouth, as well as by applying electric current. X-rays and MRI are able to determine the extent of soft tissue, mandibular and dental trauma.

3. *Chest and abdomen*

183. Examination of the trunk, in addition to noting lesions of the skin, should be directed towards detecting regions of pain, tenderness or discomfort that would reflect underlying injuries of the musculature, ribs or abdominal organs. The examiner must consider the possibility of intramuscular, retroperitoneal and intra-abdominal haematomas, as well as laceration or rupture of an internal organ. Ultrasonography, CT and bone scintigraphy should be used, when realistically available, to confirm such injuries. Routine examination of the cardiovascular system, lungs and abdomen should be performed in the usual manner. Pre-existing respiratory disorders are likely to be aggravated in custody, and new respiratory disorders frequently develop.

4. *Musculoskeletal system*

184. Complaints of musculoskeletal aches and pains are very common in survivors of torture.[75] They may be the result of repeated beatings, suspension, other positional torture or the general physical environment of detention.[76] They may also be somatic (see chapter VI, sect. B.2). While they are non-specific, they should be documented. They often respond well to sympathetic physiotherapy.[77] Physical examination of the skeleton should include testing for mobility of joints, the spine and the extremities. Pain with motion, contracture, strength, evidence of compartment syndrome, fractures with or without deformity and dislocations should all be noted. Suspected dislocations, fractures and osteomyelitis should be evaluated with radiographs. For suspected osteomyelitis, routine radiographs should be taken, followed by three-phase bone scintigraphy. Injuries to tendons, ligaments and muscles are best evaluated with MRI, but arthrography can also be performed. In the acute stage, this can detect haemorrhage and possible muscle tears. Muscles usually heal completely without scarring; thus, later imaging studies will be negative. Under MRI and CT, denervated muscles and chronic compartment

syndrome will be imaged as muscle fibrosis. Bone bruises can be detected by MRI or scintigraphy. Bone bruises usually heal without leaving traces.

5. *Genito-urinary system*

185. Genital examination should be performed only with the consent of the patient and, if necessary, should be postponed to a later examination. A chaperone must be present if the examining physician's gender is different from that of the patient. For more information, see chapter IV, sect. J. See section D.8 below for further information regarding examination of victims of sexual assault. Ultrasonography and dynamic scintigraphy can be used for detecting genito-urinary trauma.

6. *Central and peripheral nervous systems*

186. The neurological examination should evaluate the cranial nerves, sensory organs and peripheral nervous system, checking for both motor and sensory neuropathies related to possible trauma, vitamin deficiencies or disease. Cognitive ability and mental status must also be evaluated (see chapter VI, sect. C). In patients who report being suspended, special emphasis on examination for brachial plexopathy (asymmetrical hand strength, wrist drop, arm weakness with variable sensory and tendon reflexes) is necessary. Radiculopathies, other neuropathies, cranial nerve deficits, hyperalgesia, parasthesias, hyperaesthesia, change in position, temperature sensation, motor function, gait and coordination may all result from trauma associated with torture. In patients with a history of dizziness and vomiting, a vestibular examination should be conducted, and evidence of nystagmus noted. Radiological evaluation should include MRI or CT. MRI is preferred over CT for radiological evaluation of the brain and posterior fossae.

D. Examination and evaluation following specific forms of torture

187. The following discussion is not meant to be an exhaustive discussion of all forms of torture, but it is intended to describe in more detail the medical aspects of many of the more common forms of torture. For each lesion and for the overall pattern of lesions, the physician should indicate the degree of consistency between it and the attribution given by the patient. The following terms are generally used:

(*a*) Not consistent: the lesion could not have been caused by the trauma described;

(*b*) Consistent with: the lesion could have been caused by the trauma described, but it is non-specific and there are many other possible causes;

(*c*) Highly consistent: the lesion could have been caused by the trauma described, and there are few other possible causes;

(*d*) Typical of: this is an appearance that is usually found with this type of trauma, but there are other possible causes;

[75] See footnote 73 above.

[76] D. Forrest, "Examination for the late physical after-effects of torture", *Journal of Clinical Forensic Medicine*, vol. 6 (1999), pp. 4-13.

[77] See footnote 73 above.

(e) Diagnostic of: this appearance could not have been caused in any way other than that described.

188. Ultimately, it is the overall evaluation of all lesions and not the consistency of each lesion with a particular form of torture that is important in assessing the torture story (see chapter IV, sect. G, for a list of torture methods).

1. *Beatings and other forms of blunt trauma*

(a) *Skin damage*

189. Acute lesions are often characteristic of torture, because they show a pattern of inflicted injury that differs from non-inflicted injuries, for example, their shape, repetition, distribution on the body. Since most lesions heal within about six weeks of torture, leaving no scars or non-specific scars, a characteristic history of the acute lesions and their development until healing might be the only support for an allegation of torture. Permanent changes in the skin due to blunt trauma are infrequent, non-specific and usually without diagnostic significance. A sequel of blunt violence, which is diagnostic of prolonged application of tight ligatures, is a linear zone extending circularly around the arm or leg, usually at the wrist or ankle. This zone contains few hairs or hair follicles, and this is probably a form of cicatricial alopecia. No differential diagnosis in the form of a spontaneous skin disease exists, and it is difficult to imagine any trauma of this nature occurring in everyday life.

190. Among acute lesions, abrasions resulting from superficial scraping lesions of the skin may appear as scratches, brush-burn type lesions or larger scraped lesions. At times, abrasions may show a pattern that reflects the contours of the instrument or surface that inflicted the injury. Repeated or deep abrasions may create areas of hypo or hyperpigmentation, depending on skin type. This occurs on the inside of the wrists if the hands have been tied together tightly.

191. Contusions and bruises are areas of haemorrhage into soft tissue due to the rupture of blood vessels from blunt trauma. The extent and severity of a contusion depend not only on the amount of force applied but also on the structure and vascularity of the contused tissue. Contusions occur more readily in areas of thin skin overlying bone or in fatty areas. Many medical conditions, including vitamin and other nutritional deficiencies, may be associated with easy bruising or purpura. Contusions and abrasions indicate that blunt force has been applied to a particular area. The absence of a bruise or abrasion, however, does not indicate that there was no blunt force to that area. Contusions may be patterned, reflecting the contours of the inflicting instrument. For instance, rail-shaped bruising may occur when an instrument, such as a truncheon or cane, has been used. The shape of the object may be inferred from the shape of the bruise. As contusions resolve, they undergo a series of colour changes. Most bruises initially appear dark blue, purple or crimson. As the haemoglobin in the bruise breaks down, the colour gradually changes to violet, green, dark yellow or pale yellow and then disappears. It is very difficult, however, to date accurately the occurrence of contusions. In some

skin types, this can lead to hyperpigmentation, which can last several years. Contusions that develop in deeper subcutaneous tissues may not appear until several days after injury, when the extravasated blood has reached the surface. In cases of an allegation but an absence of a contusion, the victim should be re-examined after several days. It should be taken into consideration that the final position and shape of bruises bear no relationship to the original trauma and that some lesions may have faded by the time of re-examination.[78]

192. Lacerations, a tearing or crushing of the skin and underlying soft tissues by the pressure of blunt force, develop easily on the protruding parts of the body, since the skin is compressed between the blunt object and the bone surface under the subdermal tissues. However, with sufficient force the skin can be torn on any part of the body. Asymmetrical scars, scars in unusual locations and a diffuse spread of scarring all suggest deliberate injury.[79]

193. Scars resulting from whipping represent healed lacerations. These scars are depigmented and often hypertrophic, surrounded by narrow, hyperpigmented stripes. The only differential diagnosis is plant dermatitis, but this is dominated by hyperpigmentation and shorter scars. By contrast, symmetrical, atrophic, depigmented linear changes of the abdomen, axillae and legs, which are sometimes claimed to be torture sequelae, represent striae distensae and are not normally related to torture.[80]

194. Burning is the form of torture that most frequently leaves permanent changes in the skin. Sometimes, these changes may be of diagnostic value. Cigarette burns often leave 5-10-millimetre-long, circular or ovoid, macular scars with a hyper or a hypopigmented centre and a hyperpigmented, relatively indistinct periphery. The burning away of tattoos with cigarettes has also been reported in relation to torture. The characteristic shape of the resulting scar and any tattoo remnants will help in the diagnosis.[81] Burning with hot objects produces markedly atrophic scars which reflect the shape of the instrument and which are sharply demarcated with narrow hypertrophic or hyperpigmented marginal zones corresponding to an initial zone of inflammation. This may, for instance, be seen after burning with an electrically heated metal rod or a gas lighter. It is difficult to make a differential diagnosis if many scars are present. Spontaneously occurring inflammatory processes lack the characteristic marginal zone and only rarely show a pronounced loss of tissue. Burning may result in hypertrophic or keloid scars as is the case following a burn produced by burning rubber.

195. When the nail matrix is burnt, subsequent growth produces striped, thin, deformed nails, sometimes broken up in longitudinal segments. If a nail has been pulled off, an overgrowth of tissue may be produced from

[78] S. Gürpinar and S. Korur Fincanci, "Insan Haklari Ihlalleri *ve* Hekim Sorumluluğu" (Human rights violations and responsibility of the physician), *Birinci Basamak İçin Adli Tip El Kitabi* (Handbook of Forensic Medicine for General Practitioners) (Ankara, Turkish Medical Association, 1999).

[79] See footnote 73 above.

[80] L. Danielsen, "Skin changes after torture", *Torture*, vol. 2, supplement 1 (1992), pp. 27-28.

[81] Ibid.

the proximal nail fold, resulting in the formation of pterygium. Changes in the nail caused by *Lichen planus* constitute the only relevant differential diagnosis, but they will usually be accompanied by widespread skin injury. On the other hand, fungus infections are characterized by thickened, yellowish, crumbling nails, different from the above changes.

196. Sharp trauma wounds are produced when the skin is cut with a sharp object, such as a knife, bayonet or broken glass and include stab wounds, incised or cut wounds and puncture wounds. The acute appearance is usually easy to distinguish from the irregular and torn appearance of lacerations and scars found upon later examination that may be distinctive. Regular patterns of small incisional scars could be due to traditional healers.[82] If pepper or other noxious substances are applied to open wounds, the scars may become hypertrophic. An asymmetrical pattern and different sizes of scars are probably significant in the diagnosis of torture.

(b) *Fractures*

197. Fractures produce a loss of bone integrity due to the effect of a blunt mechanical force on various vector planes. A direct fracture occurs at the site of impact or at the site where the force was applied. The location, contour and other characteristics of a fracture reflect the nature and direction of the applied force. It is sometimes possible to distinguish fracture inflicted from accidental injury by the radiological appearance of the fracture. Radiographic dating of relatively recent fractures should be done by an experienced trauma radiologist. Speculative judgements should be avoided in the evaluations of the nature and age of blunt traumatic lesions, since a lesion may vary according to the age, sex, tissue characteristics, the condition and health of the patient and the severity of the trauma. For example, well-conditioned, muscularly fit, younger individuals are more resistant to bruising than frail, older individuals.

(c) *Head trauma*

198. Head trauma is one of the most common forms of torture. In cases of recurring head trauma, even if not always of serious dimensions, cortical atrophy and diffuse axonal damage can be expected. In cases of trauma caused by falls, countercoup (location in opposition to the trauma) lesions of the brain may be observed. Whereas in cases of direct trauma, contusions of the brain may be observed directly under the region in which the trauma is inflicted. Scalp bruises are frequently invisible externally unless there is swelling. Bruises may be difficult to see in dark-skinned individuals, but will be tender upon palpation.

199. Having been exposed to blows to the head, a torture survivor may complain of continuous headaches. These are often somatic or may be referred from the neck (see section C above). The victim may claim to suffer pain when touched in that region, and diffuse or local fullness or increased firmness may be observed by means of palpation of the scalp. Scars can be observed in cases where there have been lacerations of the scalp. Headaches may

be the initial symptom of an expanding subdural haematoma. They may be associated with the acute onset of mental status changes, and a CT scan must be performed urgently. Soft tissue swelling or haemorrhage will usually be detected with CT or MRI. It may also be appropriate to arrange psychological or neuropsychological assessment (see chapter VI, sect. C.4).

200. Violent shaking as a form of torture may produce cerebral injury without leaving any external marks, although bruises may be present on the upper chest or shoulders where the victim or his clothing has been grabbed. At its most extreme, shaking can produce injuries identical to those seen in the shaken baby syndrome: cerebral oedema, subdural haematoma and retinal haemorrhages. More commonly, victims complain of recurrent headaches, disorientation or mental status changes. Shaking episodes are usually brief, only a few minutes or less, but may be repeated many times over a period of days or weeks.

(d) *Chest and abdominal trauma*

201. Rib fractures are a frequent consequence of beatings to the chest. If displaced, they can be associated with lacerations of the lung and possible pneumothorax. Fractures of the vertebral pedicles may result from direct use of blunt force.

202. In cases of acute abdominal trauma, the physical examination should seek evidence of abdominal organ and urinary tract injury. However, the examination is often negative. Gross haematuria is the most significant indication of kidney contusion. Peritoneal lavage may detect occult abdominal haemorrhage. Free abdominal fluid detected by CT after peritoneal lavage may be from the lavage or haemorrhage; thus invalidating the finding. On a CT, acute abdominal haemorrhage is usually isointense or reveals water density unlike acute central nervous system (CNS) haemorrhage, which is hyperintense. Organ injury may be present as free air, extraluminal fluid or areas of low attenuation, which may represent oedema, contusion, haemorrhage or a laceration. Peripancreatic oedema is one of the signs of acute traumatic and nontraumatic pancreatitis. Ultrasound is particularly useful in detecting subcapsular haematomas of the spleen. Renal failure due to crush syndrome may be acute after severe beatings. Renal hypertension can be a late complication of renal injury.

2. *Beatings to the feet*

203. *Falanga* is the most common term for repeated application of blunt trauma to the feet (or more rarely to the hands or hips), usually applied with a truncheon, a length of pipe or similar weapon. The most severe complication of *falanga* is closed compartment syndrome, which can cause muscle necrosis, vascular obstruction or gangrene of the distal portion of the foot or toes. Permanent deformities of the feet are uncommon but do occur, as do fractures of the carpal, metacarpal and phalanges. Because the injuries are usually confined to soft tissue, CT or MRI are the preferred methods for radiological documentation of the injury, but it must be emphasized that physical examination in the acute phase should be

---

[82] See footnote 76 above.

diagnostic. *Falanga* may produce chronic disability. Walking may be painful and difficult. The tarsal bones may be fixed (spastic) or have increased motion. Squeezing the plantar (sole) of the foot and dorsiflexion of the great toe may produce pain. On palpation, the entire length of the plantar aponeurosis may be tender and the distal attachments of the aponeurosis may be torn, partly at the base of the proximal phalanges, partly at the skin. The aponeurosis will not tighten normally, making walking difficult and muscle fatigue may follow. Passive extension of the big toe may reveal whether the aponeurosis has been torn. If it is intact, the beginning of tension in the aponeurosis should be felt on palpation when the toe is dorsiflexed to 20 degrees; maximum normal extension is about 70 degrees. Higher values suggest injury to the attachments of the aponeurosis.[83, 84, 85, 86] On the other hand, limited dorsiflexion and pain on hyperextension of the large toe are findings of *Hallux rigidus*, which results from dorsal osteophyte at the first metatarsal head and/or base of the proximal phalanx.

204. Numerous complications and syndromes can occur:

(*a*) Closed compartment syndrome. This is the most severe complication. An oedema in a closed compartment results in vascular obstruction and muscle necrosis, which may result in fibrosis, contracture or gangrene in the distal foot or toes. It is usually diagnosed by measuring pressures in the compartment;

(*b*) Crushed heel and anterior footpads. The elastic pads under the calcaneus and proximal phalanxes are crushed during *falanga*, either directly or as a result of oedema associated with the trauma. Also, the connective tissue bands that extend through adipose tissue and connect bone to the skin are torn. Adipose tissue is deprived of its blood supply and atrophies. The cushioning effect is lost and the feet no longer absorb the stresses produced by walking;

(*c*) Rigid and irregular scars involving the skin and subcutaneous tissues of the foot after the application of *falanga*. In a normal foot, the dermal and sub-dermal tissues are connected to the planter aponeurosis through tight connective tissue bands. However, these bands can be partially or completely destroyed due to the oedema that ruptures the bands after exposure to *falanga*;

(*d*) Rupture of the plantar aponeurosis and tendons of the foot. An oedema in the post-*falanga* period may rupture these structures. When the supportive function necessary for the arch of the foot disappears, the act of walking becomes more difficult and foot muscles, especially the *quadratus plantaris longus*, are excessively forced;

(*e*) Planter fasciitis. May occur as a further complication of this injury. In cases of *falanga*, irritation is often present throughout the whole aponeurosis, causing chronic aponeurositis. Studies on the subject have shown that in prisoners released after 15 years of detention and who claimed to have been subjected to *falanga* application when first arrested, positive bone scans of hyperactive points in the calcaneus or metatarsal bones were observed.[87]

205. Radiological methods such as MRI, CT scan and ultrasound can often confirm cases of trauma occurring as a result of the application of *falanga*. Positive radiological findings may also be secondary to other diseases or trauma. Routine radiographs are recommended as the initial examination. MRI is the preferred radiological examination for detecting soft tissue injury. MRI or scintigraphy can detect bone injury in the form of a bruise, which may not be detected by routine radiographs or CT.[88]

3. *Suspension*

206. Suspension is a common form of torture that can produce extreme pain, but which leaves little, if any, visible evidence of injury. A person still in custody may be reluctant to admit to being tortured, but the finding of peripheral neurological deficits, diagnostic of brachial plexopathy, virtually proves the diagnosis of suspension torture. Suspension can be applied in various forms:

(*a*) Cross suspension. Applied by spreading the arms and tying them to a horizontal bar;

(*b*) Butchery suspension. Applied by fixation of hands upwards, either together or one by one;

(*c*) Reverse butchery suspension. Applied by fixation of feet upward and the head downward;

(*d*) "Palestinian" suspension. Applied by suspending the victim with the forearms bound together behind the back, the elbows flexed 90 degrees and the forearms tied to a horizontal bar. Alternatively, the prisoner is suspended from a ligature tied around the elbows or wrists with the arms behind the back;

(*e*) "Parrot perch" suspension. Applied by suspending a victim by the flexed knees from a bar passed below the popliteal region, usually while the wrists are tied to the ankles.

207. Suspension may last from 15 to 20 minutes to several hours. "Palestinian" suspension may produce permanent brachial plexus injury in a short period. The "parrot perch" may produce tears in the cruciate ligaments of the knees. Victims will often be beaten while suspended or otherwise abused. In the chronic phase, it is usual for pain and tenderness around the shoulder joints to persist,

[83] G. Sklyv, "Physical sequelae of torture", in *Torture and Its Consequences: Current Treatment Approaches*, M. Başoğlu, ed. (Cambridge, Cambridge University Press, 1992), pp. 38-55.

[84] See footnote 76.

[85] K. Prip, L. Tived, N. Holten, *Physiotherapy for Torture Survivors: A Basic Introduction* (Copenhagen, International Rehabilitation Council for Torture Victims, 1995).

[86] F. Bojsen-Moller and K. E. Flagstad, "Plantar aponeurosis and internal architecture of the ball of the foot", *Journal of Anatomy*, vol. 121 (1976), pp. 599-611.

[87] V. Lök and others, "Bone scintigraphy as clue to previous torture", *The Lancet*, vol. 337, No. 8745 (1991), pp. 846-847. See also M. Tunca and V. Lök, "Bone scintigraphy in screening of torture survivors", *The Lancet*, vol. 352, No. 9143 (1998), p. 1859.

[88] See footnotes 76 and 83 and V. Lök and others, "Bone scintigraphy as an evidence of previous torture", *Treatment and Rehabilitation Center Report of the Human Rights Foundation of Turkey* (Ankara, 1994), pp. 91-96.

as the lifting of weight and rotation, especially internal, will cause severe pain many years later. Complications in the acute period following suspension include weakness of the arms or hands, pain and parasthesias, numbness, insensitivity to touch, superficial pain and tendon reflex loss. Intense deep pain may mask muscle weakness. In the chronic phase, weakness may continue and progress to muscle wasting. Numbness and, more frequently, parasthesia are present. Raising the arms or lifting weight may cause pain, numbness or weakness. In addition to neurologic injury, there may be tears of the ligaments of the shoulder joints, dislocation of the scapula and muscle injury in the shoulder region. On visual inspection of the back, a "winged scapula" (prominent vertebral border of the scapula) may be observed with injury to the long thoracic nerve or dislocation of the scapula.

208.   Neurologic injury is usually asymmetrical in the arms. Brachial plexus injury manifests itself in motor, sensory and reflex dysfunction.

(*a*) Motor examination. Asymmetrical muscle weakness, more prominent distally, is the most expected finding. Acute pain may make the examination for muscle strength difficult to interpret. If the injury is severe, muscle atrophy may be seen in the chronic phase;

(*b*) Sensory examination. Complete loss of sensation or parasthesias along the sensory nerve pathways is common. Positional perception, two-point discrimination, pinprick evaluation and perception of heat and cold should all be tested. If at least three weeks later, deficiency or reflex loss or decrease is present, appropriate electrophysiological studies should be performed by a neurologist experienced in the use and interpretation of these methodologies;

(*c*) Reflex examination. Reflex loss, a decrease in reflexes or a difference between the two extremities may be present. In "Palestinian" suspension, even though both brachial plexi are subjected to trauma, asymmetric plexopathy may develop due to the manner in which the torture victim has been suspended, depending on which arm is placed in a superior position or the method of binding. Although research suggests that brachial plexopathies are usually unilateral, that is at variance with experience in the context of torture, where bilateral injury is common.

209.   Among the shoulder region tissues, the brachial plexus is the structure most sensitive to traction injury. "Palestinian" suspension creates brachial plexus damage due to forced posterior extension of the arms. As observed in the classical type of "Palestinian" suspension, when the body is suspended with the arms in posterior hyperextension, typically the lower plexus and then the middle and upper plexus fibres, if the force on the plexus is severe enough, are damaged, respectively. If the suspension is of a "crucifixion" type, but does not include hyperextension, the middle plexus fibres are likely to be the first ones damaged due to hyperabduction. Brachial plexus injuries may be categorized as follows:

(*a*) Damage to the lower plexus. Deficiencies are localized in the forearm and hand muscles. Sensory deficiencies may be observed on the forearm and at the fourth and fifth fingers of the hand's medial side in an ulnar nerve distribution;

(*b*) Damage to the middle plexus. Forearm, elbow and finger extensor muscles are affected. Pronation of the forearm and radial flexion of the hand may be weak. Sensory deficiency is found on the forearm and on the dorsal aspects of the first, second and third fingers of the hand in a radial nerve distribution. Triceps reflexes may be lost;

(*c*) Damage to the upper plexus. Shoulder muscles are especially affected. Abduction of the shoulder, axial rotation and forearm pronation-supination may be deficient. Sensory deficiency is noted in the deltoid region and may extend to the arm and outer parts of the forearm.

4.   *Other positional torture*

210.   There are many forms of positional torture, all of which tie or restrain the victim in contorted, hyperextended or other unnatural positions, which cause severe pain and may produce injuries to ligaments, tendons, nerves and blood vessels. Characteristically, these forms of torture leave few, if any, external marks or radiological findings, despite subsequent frequently severe chronic disability.

211.   All positional torture is directed towards tendons, joints and muscles. There are various methods: "parrot suspension", "banana stand" or the classic "banana tie" over a chair just on the ground, or on a motorcycle, forced standing, forced standing on a single foot, prolonged standing with arms and hands stretched high on a wall, prolonged forced squatting and forced immobilization in a small cage. In accordance with the characteristics of these positions, complaints are characterized as pain in a region of the body, limitation of joint movement, back pain, pain in the hands or cervical parts of the body and swelling of the lower legs. The same principles of neurologic and musculoskeletal examination apply to these forms of positional torture as apply to suspension. MRI is the preferred radiologic modality for evaluation of injuries associated with all forms of positional torture.

5.   *Electric shock torture*

212.   Electric current is transmitted through electrodes placed on any part of the body. The most common areas are the hands, feet, fingers, toes, ears, nipples, mouth, lips and genital area. The power source may be a hand-cranked or combustion generator, wall source, stun gun, cattle prod or other electric device. Electric current follows the shortest route between the two electrodes. The symptoms that occur when electric current is applied have this characteristic. For example, if electrodes are placed on a toe of the right foot and on the genital region, there will be pain, muscle contraction and cramps in the right thigh and calf muscles. Excruciating pain will be felt in the genital region. Since all muscles along the route of the electric current are tetanically contracted, dislocation of the shoulder, lumbar and cervical radiculopathies may be observed when the current is moderately high. However, the type, time of application, current and voltage of the energy used cannot be determined with certainty upon physical examination of the victim. Torturers often use water or gels in order to increase the efficiency of the tor-

40

ture, expand the entrance point of the electric current on the body and prevent detectable electric burns. Trace electrical burns are usually a reddish brown circular lesion from 1 to 3 millimetres in diameter, usually without inflammation, which may result in a hyperpigmented scar. Skin surfaces must be carefully examined because the lesions are not often easily discernible. The decision to biopsy recent lesions to prove their origin is controversial. Electrical burns may produce specific histologic changes, but these are not always present, and the absence of change in no way mitigates against the lesion being an electrical burn. The decision must be made on a case-by-case basis as to whether or not the pain and discomfort associated with a skin biopsy can be justified by the potential results of the procedure (see annex II, sect. 2).

6. *Dental torture*

213.   Dental torture may be in the form of breaking or extracting teeth or through application of electrical current to the teeth. It may result in a loss or breaking of the teeth, swelling of the gums, bleeding, pain, gingivitis, stomatitis, mandibular fractures or loss of fillings from teeth. Temporomandibular joint syndrome will produce pain in the temporomandibular joint, limitation of jaw movement and, in some cases, subluxation of this joint due to muscle spasms occurring as a result of the electrical current or blows to the face.

7. *Asphyxiation*

214.   Near asphyxiation by suffocation is an increasingly common method of torture. It usually leaves no mark, and recuperation is rapid. This method of torture was so widely used in Latin America, that its name in Spanish, *submarino*, has become part of human rights vocabulary. Normal respiration might be prevented through such methods as covering the head with a plastic bag, closure of the mouth and nose, pressure or ligature around the neck or forced aspiration of dust, cement, hot peppers, etc. This is also known as "dry *submarino*". Various complications might develop, such as petechiae of the skin, nosebleeds, bleeding from the ears, congestion of the face, infections in the mouth and acute or chronic respiratory problems. Forcible immersion of the head in water, often contaminated with urine, faeces, vomit or other impurities, may result in near drowning or drowning. Aspiration of the water into the lungs may lead to pneumonia. This form of torture is called "wet *submarino*". In hanging or in other ligature asphyxiation, patterned abrasions or contusions can often be found on the neck. The hyoid bone and laryngeal cartilage may be fractured by partial strangulation or from blows to the neck.

8. *Sexual torture including rape*

215.   Sexual torture begins with forced nudity, which in many countries is a constant factor in torture situations. An individual is never as vulnerable as when naked and helpless. Nudity enhances the psychological terror of every aspect of torture, as there is always the background of potential abuse, rape or sodomy. Furthermore, verbal sexual threats, abuse and mocking are also part of sexual torture, as they enhance the humiliation and its degrading aspects, all part and parcel of the procedure. The groping of women is traumatic in all cases and is considered to be torture.

216.   There are some differences between sexual torture of men and sexual torture of women, but several issues apply to both. Rape is always associated with the risk of developing sexually transmitted diseases, particularly human immunodeficiency virus (HIV).[89] Currently, the only effective prophylaxis against HIV must be taken within hours of the incident, and it is not generally available in countries where torture occurs routinely. In most cases, there will be a lewd sexual component, and in other cases torture is targeted at the genitals. Electricity and blows are generally targeted on the genitals in men, with or without additional anal torture. The resulting physical trauma is enhanced by verbal abuse. There are often threats of loss of masculinity to men and consequent loss of respect in society. Prisoners may be placed naked in cells with family members, friends or total strangers, breaking cultural taboos. This can be made worse by the absence of privacy when using toilet facilities. Additionally, prisoners may be forced to abuse each other sexually, which can be particularly difficult to cope with emotionally. The fear of potential rape among women, given profound cultural stigma associated with rape, can add to the trauma. Not to be neglected are the trauma of potential pregnancy, which males, obviously, do not experience, the fear of losing virginity and the fear of not being able to have children (even if the rape can be hidden from a potential husband and the rest of society).

217.   If in cases of sexual abuse the victim does not wish the event to be known due to sociocultural pressures or personal reasons, the physician who carries out the medical examination, investigative agencies and the courts have an obligation to cooperate in maintaining the victim's privacy. Establishing a rapport with torture survivors who have recently been sexually assaulted requires special psychological education and appropriate psychological support. Any treatment that would increase the psychological trauma of a torture survivor should be avoided. Before starting the examination, permission must be obtained from the individual for any kind of examination, and this should be confirmed by the victim before the more intimate parts of the examination. The individual should be informed about the importance of the examination and its possible findings in a clear and comprehensible manner.

(a)   *Review of symptoms*

218.   A thorough history of the alleged assault should be recorded as described earlier in this manual (see section B above). There are, however, some specific questions that are relevant only to an allegation of sexual abuse. These seek to elicit current symptoms resulting from a recent assault, for example bleeding, vaginal or anal discharge and location of pain, bruises or sores. In cases of sexual assault in the past, questions should be directed to ongoing symptoms that resulted from the

---

[89] I. Lunde and J. Ortmann, "Sexual torture and the treatment of its consequences", *Torture and Its Consequences, Current Treatment Approaches*, M. Başoğlu, ed. (Cambridge, Cambridge University Press, 1992), pp. 310-331.

assault, such as urinary frequency, incontinence or dysuria, irregularity of menstruation, subsequent history of pregnancy, abortion or vaginal haemorrhage, problems with sexual activity, including intercourse and anal pain, bleeding, constipation or incontinence.

219. Ideally, there should be adequate physical and technical facilities for appropriate examination of survivors of sexual violation by a team of experienced psychiatrists, psychologists, gynaecologists and nurses, who are trained in the treatment of survivors of sexual torture. An additional purpose of the consultation after sexual assault is to offer support, advice and, if appropriate, reassurance. This should cover issues such as sexually transmitted diseases, HIV, pregnancy, if the victim is a woman, and permanent physical damage, because torturers often tell victims that they will never normally function sexually again, which can become a self-fulfilling prophecy.

(b) *Examination following a recent assault*

220. It is rare that a victim of rape during torture is released while it is still possible to identify acute signs of the assault. In these cases, there are many issues to be aware of that may impede the medical evaluation. Recently assaulted victims may be troubled and confused about seeking medical or legal help due to their fears, sociocultural concerns or the destructive nature of the abuse. In such cases, a doctor should explain to the victim all possible medical and judicial options and should act in accordance with the victim's wishes. The duties of the physician include obtention of voluntary informed consent for the examination, recording of all medical findings of abuse and obtention of samples for forensic examination. Whenever possible, the examination should be performed by an expert in documenting sexual assault. Otherwise, the examining physician should speak to an expert or consult a standard text on clinical forensic medicine.[90] When the physician is of a different gender from the victim, he or she should be offered the opportunity of having a chaperone of the same gender in the room. If an interpreter is used, then the interpreter may also fulfil the role of the chaperone. Given the sensitive nature of investigation into sexual assaults, a relative of the victim is not normally an ideal person to use in this role (see chapter IV, sect. I). The patient should be comfortable and relaxed before the examination. A thorough physical examination should be performed, including meticulous documentation of all physical findings, including size, location and colour, and, whenever possible, these findings should be photographed and evidence collected of specimens from the examination.

221. The physical examination should not initially be directed to the genital area. Any deformities should be noted. Particular attention must be given to ensure a thorough examination of the skin, looking for cutaneous lesions that could have resulted from an assault. These include bruises, lacerations, ecchymoses and petechiae from sucking or biting. This may help the patient to be more relaxed for a complete examination. When genital lesions are minimal, lesions located on other parts of the

body may be the most significant evidence of an assault. Even during examination of the female genitalia immediately after rape, there is identifiable damage in less than 50 per cent of the cases. Anal examination of men and women after anal rape shows lesions in less than 30 per cent of cases. Clearly, where relatively large objects have been used to penetrate the vagina or anus, the probability of identifiable damage is much greater.

222. Where a forensic laboratory is available, the facility should be contacted before the examination to discuss which types of specimen can be tested, and, therefore, which samples should be taken and how. Many laboratories provide kits to permit physicians to take all the necessary samples from individuals alleging sexual assault. If there is no laboratory available, it may still be worthwhile to obtain wet swabs and dry them later in the air. These samples can be used later for DNA testing. Sperm can be identified for up to five days from samples taken with a deep vaginal swab and after up to three days using a rectal sample. Strict precautions must be taken to prevent allegations of cross-contamination when samples have been taken from several different victims, particularly if they are taken from alleged perpetrators. There must be complete protection and documentation of the chain of custody for all forensic samples.

(c) *Examination after the immediate phase*

223. Where the alleged assault occurred more than a week earlier and there are no signs of bruises or lacerations, there is less immediacy in conducting a pelvic examination. Time can be taken to try to find the most qualified person to document findings and the best environment in which to interview the individual. However, it may still be beneficial to photograph residual lesions properly, if this is possible.

224. The background should be recorded as described above, then examination and documentation of the general physical findings. In women who have delivered babies before the rape, and particularly in those who have delivered them afterwards, pathognomonic findings are not likely, although an experienced female physician can tell a considerable amount from the demeanour of a woman when she is describing her history.[91] It may take some time before the individual is willing to discuss those aspects of the torture that he or she finds most embarrassing. Similarly, patients may wish to postpone the more intimate parts of the examination to a subsequent consultation, if time and circumstances permit.

(d) *Follow-up*

225. Many infectious diseases can be transmitted by sexual assault, including sexually transmitted diseases such as gonorrhoea, chlamydia, syphilis, HIV, hepatitis B and C, herpes simplex and *Condyloma acuminatum* (venereal warts), vulvovaginitis associated with sexual abuse, such as trichomoniasis, *Moniliasis vaginitis*, *Gardnerella vaginitis* and *Enterobius vermicularis* (pinworms), as well as urinary tract infections.

---

[90] See J. Howitt and D. Rogers, "Adult sexual offences and related matters", *Journal of Clinical Forensic Medicine*, W. D. S. McLay, ed. (London, Greenwich Medical Media, 1996), pp. 193-218.

[91] G. Hinshelwood, *Gender-based persecution* (Toronto, United Nations Expert Group Meeting on Gender-based Persecution, 1997).

226. Appropriate laboratory tests and treatment should be prescribed in all cases of sexual abuse. In the case of gonorrhoea and chlamydia, concomitant infection of the anus or oropharynx should be considered at least for examination purposes. Initial cultures and serologic tests should be obtained in cases of sexual assault, and appropriate therapy initiated. Sexual dysfunction is common among survivors of torture, particularly among victims who have suffered sexual torture or rape, but not exclusively. Symptoms may be physical or psychological in origin or a combination of both and include:

(i) Aversion to members of the opposite sex or decreased interest in sexual activity;

(ii) Fear of sexual activity because a sexual partner will know that the victim has been sexually abused or fear of having been damaged sexually. Torturers may have threatened this and instilled fear of homosexuality in men who have been anally abused. Some heterosexual men have had an erection and, on occasion, have ejaculated during non-consensual anal intercourse. They should be reassured that this is a physiological response;

(iii) Inability to trust a sexual partner;

(iv) Disturbance in sexual arousal and erectile dysfunction;

(v) Dyspareunia (painful sexual intercourse in women) or infertility due to acquired sexually transmitted disease, direct trauma to reproductive organs or poorly performed abortions of pregnancies following rape.

(e) *Genital examination of women*

227. In many cultures, it is completely unacceptable to penetrate the vagina of a woman who is a virgin with anything, including a speculum, finger or swab. If the woman demonstrates clear evidence of rape on external inspection, it may be unnecessary to conduct an internal pelvic examination. Genital examination findings may include:

(i) Small lacerations or tears of the vulva. These may be acute and are caused by excessive stretching. They normally heal completely, but, if repeatedly traumatized, there may be scarring;

(ii) Abrasions of the female genitalia. Abrasions can be caused by contact with rough objects such as fingernails or rings;

(iii) Vaginal lacerations. These are rare, but, if present, may be associated with atrophy of the tissues or previous surgery. They cannot be differentiated from incisions caused by inserted sharp objects.

228. It is rare to find any physical evidence when examining female genitalia more than one week after an assault. Later on, when the woman may have had subsequent sexual activity, whether consensual or not, or given birth, it may be almost impossible to attribute any findings to a specific incident of alleged abuse. Therefore, the most significant component of a medical evaluation may be the examiner's assessment of background information (for example, correlation between allegations of abuse and acute injuries observed by the individual) and demeanour of the individual, bearing in mind the cultural context of the woman's experience.

(f) *Genital examination of men*

229. Men who have been subjected to torture of the genital region, including the crushing, wringing or pulling of the scrotum or direct trauma to that region, usually complain of pain and sensitivity in the acute period. Hyperaemia, marked swelling and ecchymosis can be observed. The urine may contain a large number of erythrocytes and leucocytes. If a mass is detected, it should be determined whether it is a hydrocele, haematocele or inguinal hernia. In the case of an inguinal hernia, the examiner cannot palpate the spermatic cord above the mass. With a hydrocele or a haematocele, normal spermatic cord structures are usually palpable above the mass. A hydrocele results from excessive accumulation of fluid within the tunica vaginalis due to inflammation of the testis and its appendages or to diminished drainage secondary to lymphatic or venous obstruction in the cord or retroperitoneal space. A haematocele is an accumulation of blood within the tunica vaginalis, secondary to trauma. Unlike the hydrocele, it does not transilluminate.

230. Testicular torsion may also result from trauma to the scrotum. With this injury, the testis becomes twisted at its base, obstructing blood flow to the testis. This causes severe pain and swelling and constitutes a surgical emergency. Failure to reduce the torsion immediately will lead to infarction of the testis. Under conditions of detention, where medical care may be denied, late sequelae of this lesion may be observed.

231. Individuals who were subject to scrotal torture may suffer from chronic urinary tract infection, erectile dysfunction or atrophy of the testes. Symptoms of PTSD are not uncommon. In the chronic phase, it may be impossible to distinguish between scrotal pathology caused by torture and that caused by other disease processes. Failure to discover any physical abnormalities on full urological examination suggests that urinary symptoms, impotence or other sexual problems may be explained on psychological grounds. Scars on the skin of the scrotum and penis may be very difficult to visualize. For this reason, the absence of scarring at these specific locations does not demonstrate the absence of torture. On the other hand, the presence of scarring usually indicates that substantial trauma was sustained.

(g) *Examination of the anal region*

232. After anal rape or insertion of objects into the anus of either gender, pain and bleeding can occur for days or weeks. This often leads to constipation, which can be exacerbated by the poor diet in many places of detention. Gastrointestinal and urinary symptoms may also occur. In the acute phase, any examination beyond visual inspection may require local or general anaesthesia and should be performed by a specialist. In the chronic phase, several symptoms may persist, and they should be investigated. There may be anal scars of unusual size or position, and these should be documented. Anal fissures may persist for many years, but it is normally impossible to

differentiate between those caused by torture and those caused by other mechanisms. On examination of the anus, the following findings should be looked for and documented:

(i) Fissures tend to be non-specific findings as they can occur in a number of "normal" situations (constipation, poor hygiene). However, when seen in an acute situation (i.e. within 72 hours) fissures are a more specific finding and can be considered evidence of penetration;

(ii) Rectal tears with or without bleeding may be noted;

(iii) Disruption of the rugal pattern may manifest as smooth fan-shaped scarring. When these scars are seen out of midline (i.e. not at 12 or 6 o'clock), they can be an indication of penetrating trauma;

(iv) Skin tags, which can be the result of healing trauma;

(iv) Purulent discharge from the anus. Cultures should be taken for gonorrhoea and chlamydia in all cases of alleged rectal penetration, regardless of whether a discharge is noted.

E. Specialized diagnostic tests

233. Diagnostic tests are not an essential part of the clinical assessment of a person alleging having been tortured. In many cases, a medical history and physical examination are sufficient. However, there are circumstances in which such tests are valuable supporting evidence. For example, where there is a legal case against members of the authorities or a claim for compensation. In these cases, a positive test might make the difference between a case succeeding or failing. Additionally, if diagnostic tests are performed for therapeutic reasons, the results should be added to the clinical report. It must be recognized that the absence of a positive diagnostic test result, as with physical findings, must not be used to suggest that torture has not occurred. There are many situations in which diagnostic tests are not available for technical reasons, but their absence should never invalidate an otherwise properly written report. It is inappropriate to use limited diagnostic facilities to document injuries for legal reasons alone, when there are greater clinical needs for those facilities (for further details, see annex II).

Chapter VI

PSYCHOLOGICAL EVIDENCE OF TORTURE

A. General considerations

1. *The central role of the psychological evaluation*

234. It is a widely held view that torture is an extraordinary life experience capable of causing a wide range of physical and psychological suffering. Most clinicians and researchers agree that the extreme nature of the torture event is powerful enough on its own to produce mental and emotional consequences, regardless of the individual's pre-torture psychological status. The psychological consequences of torture, however, occur in the context of personal attribution of meaning, personality development and social, political and cultural factors. For this reason, it cannot be assumed that all forms of torture have the same outcome. For example, the psychological consequences of a mock execution are not the same as those due to a sexual assault, and solitary confinement and isolation are not likely to produce the same effects as physical acts of torture. Likewise, one cannot assume that the effects of detention and torture on an adult will be the same as those on a child. Nevertheless, there are clusters of symptoms and psychological reactions that have been observed and documented in torture survivors with some regularity.

235. Perpetrators often attempt to justify their acts of torture and ill-treatment by the need to gather information. Such conceptualizations obscure the purpose of torture and its intended consequences. One of the central aims of torture is to reduce an individual to a position of extreme helplessness and distress that can lead to a deterioration of cognitive, emotional and behavioural functions.[92] Thus, torture is a means of attacking an individual's fundamental modes of psychological and social functioning. Under such circumstances, the torturer strives not only to incapacitate a victim physically but also to disintegrate the individual's personality. The torturer attempts to destroy a victim's sense of being grounded in a family and society as a human being with dreams, hopes and aspirations for the future. By dehumanizing and breaking the will of their victims, torturers set horrific examples for those who later come in contact with the victim. In this way, torture can break or damage the will and coherence of entire communities. In addition, torture can profoundly damage intimate relationships between spouses, parents, children, other family members and relationships between the victims and their communities.

236. It is important to recognize that not everyone who has been tortured develops a diagnosable mental illness. However, many victims experience profound emotional reactions and psychological symptoms. The main psychiatric disorders associated with torture are PTSD and major depression. While these disorders are present in the general population, their prevalence is much higher among traumatized populations. The unique cultural, social and political implications that torture has for each individual influence his or her ability to describe and speak about it. These are important factors that contribute to the impact that torture inflicts psychologically and socially and that must be considered when performing an evaluation of an individual from another culture. Cross-cultural research reveals that phenomenological or descriptive methods are the most rational approaches to use when attempting to evaluate psychological or psychiatric disorders. What is considered disordered behaviour or a disease in one culture may not be viewed as pathological in another.[93, 94, 95] Since the Second World War, progress has been made towards understanding the psychological consequences of violence. Certain psychological symptoms and clusters of symptoms have been observed and documented among survivors of torture and other types of violence.

237. In recent years, the diagnosis of PTSD has been applied to an increasingly broad array of individuals suffering from the impact of widely varying types of violence. However, the utility of this diagnosis in non-Western cultures has not been established. Nevertheless, evidence suggests that there are high rates of PTSD and depression symptoms among traumatized refugee populations from many different ethnic and cultural backgrounds.[96, 97, 98] The World Health Organization's cross-

---

[92] G. Fischer and N. F. Gurris, "Grenzverletzungen: Folter und sexuelle Traumatisierung", *Praxis der Psychotherapie–Ein integratives Lehrbuch für Psychoanalyse und Verhaltenstherapie*, W. Senf and M. Broda, eds. (Stuttgart, Thieme, 1996).

[93] A. Kleinman, "Anthropology and psychiatry: the role of culture in cross-cultural research on illness and care", paper delivered at the World Psychiatric Association regional symposium on psychiatry and its related disciplines, 1986.

[94] H. T. Engelhardt, "The concepts of health and disease", *Evaluation and Explanation in the Biomedical Sciences*, H. T. Engelhardt and S. F. Spicker, eds. (Dordrecht, D. Reidel Publishing Co., 1975), pp. 125-141.

[95] J. Westermeyer, "Psychiatric diagnosis across cultural boundaries", *American Journal of Psychiatry*, vol. 142 (7) (1985), pp. 798-805.

[96] R. F. Mollica and others, "The effect of trauma and confinement on functional health and mental health status of Cambodians living in Thailand-Cambodia border camps", *Journal of the American Medical Association (JAMA)*, vol. 270 (1993), pp. 581-586.

[97] J. D. Kinzie and others. "The prevalence of posttraumatic stress disorder and its clinical significance among Southeast Asian refugees", *American Journal of Psychiatry*, vol. 147 (7) (1990), pp. 913-917.

[98] K. Allden and others, "Burmese political dissidents in Thailand: trauma and survival among young adults in exile", *American Journal of Public Health*, vol. 86 (1996), pp. 1561-1569.

cultural study of depression provides helpful information.[99] While some symptoms may be present across different cultures, they may not be the symptoms that concern the individual the most.

2. *The context of the psychological evaluation*

238. Evaluations take place in a variety of political contexts. This results in important differences in the manner in which an evaluation should be conducted. The physician or psychologist must adapt the following guidelines to the particular situation and purpose of the evaluation (see chapter III, sect. C.2).

239. Whether or not certain questions can be asked safely will vary considerably and depends on the degree to which confidentiality and security can be ensured. For example, an examination in a prison by a visiting physician, that is limited to 15 minutes, cannot follow the same course as a forensic examination in a private office that may last for several hours. Additional problems arise when trying to assess whether psychological symptoms or behaviours are pathological or adaptive. When a person is examined while in detention or living under considerable threat or oppression, some symptoms may be adaptive. For example, diminished interest in activities and feelings of detachment or estrangement would be understandable in a person in solitary confinement. Likewise, hypervigilance and avoidance behaviours may be necessary for persons living in repressive societies.[100] The limitations of certain conditions for interviews, however, do not preclude aspiring to application of the guidelines set forth in this manual. It is especially important in difficult circumstances that governments and authorities involved be held to these standards as much as possible.

B. Psychological consequences of torture

1. *Cautionary remarks*

240. Before entering into a technical description of symptoms and psychiatric classifications, it should be noted that psychiatric classifications are generally considered to be Western medical concepts and that their application to non-Western populations presents, either implicitly or explicitly, certain difficulties. It can be argued that Western cultures suffer from an undue medicalization of psychological processes. The idea that mental suffering represents a disorder that resides in an individual and features a set of typical symptoms may be unacceptable to many members of non-Western societies. Nonetheless, there is considerable evidence of biological changes that occur in PTSD and, from that perspective,

PTSD is a diagnosable syndrome amenable to treatment biologically and psychologically.[101] As much as possible, the evaluating physician or psychologist should attempt to relate to mental suffering in the context of the individual's beliefs and cultural norms. This includes respect for the political context as well as cultural and religious beliefs. Given the severity of torture and its consequences, when performing a psychological evaluation, an attitude of informed learning should be adopted rather than one of rushing to diagnose and classify. Ideally, this attitude will communicate to the victim that his or her complaints and suffering are being recognized as real and expectable under the circumstances. In this sense, a sensitive empathic attitude may offer the victim some relief from the experience of alienation.

2. *Common psychological responses*

(a) *Re-experiencing the trauma*

241. A victim may have flashbacks or intrusive memories, in which the traumatic event is happening all over again, even while the person is awake and conscious, or recurrent nightmares, which include elements of the traumatic event in their original or symbolic form. Distress at exposure to cues that symbolize or resemble the trauma is frequently manifested by a lack of trust and fear of persons in authority, including physicians and psychologists. In countries or situations where authorities participate in human rights violations, lack of trust and fear of authority figures should not be assumed to be pathological.

(b) *Avoidance and emotional numbing*

 (i) Avoidance of any thought, conversation, activity, place or person that arouses a recollection of the trauma;

 (ii) Profound emotional constriction;

 (iii) Profound personal detachment and social withdrawal;

 (iv) Inability to recall an important aspect of the trauma.

(c) *Hyperarousal*

 (i) Difficulty either falling or staying asleep;

 (ii) Irritability or outbursts of anger;

 (iii) Difficulty concentrating;

 (iv) Hypervigilance, exaggerated startled response;

 (v) Generalized anxiety;

 (vi) Shortness of breath, sweating, dry mouth or dizziness and gastrointestinal distress.

---

[99] N. Sartorius, "Cross-cultural research on depression", *Psychopathology*, vol. 19 (2) (1987), pp. 6-11.

[100] M. A. Simpson, "What went wrong?: diagnostic and ethical problems in dealing with the effects of torture and repression in South Africa", *Beyond Trauma: Cultural and Societal Dynamics*, R. J. Kleber, C. R. Figley, B. P. R. Gersons, eds. (New York, Plenum Press, 1995), pp.188-210.

[101] M. Friedman and J. Jaranson, "The applicability of the post-traumatic stress disorder concept to refugees", *Amidst Peril and Pain: The Mental Health and Well-being of the World's Refugees*, A. Marsella and others, eds. (Washington, D. C., American Psychological Association, 1994), pp. 207-227.

(d) *Symptoms of depression*

242. The following symptoms of depression may be present: depressed mood, anhedonia (markedly diminished interest or pleasure in activities), appetite disturbance or weight loss, insomnia or hypersomnia, psychomotor agitation or retardation, fatigue and loss of energy, feelings of worthlessness and excessive guilt, difficulty paying attention, concentrating or recalling from memory, thoughts of death and dying, suicidal ideation or attempted suicide.

(e) *Damaged self-concept and foreshortened future*

243. The victim has a subjective feeling of having been irreparably damaged and having undergone an irreversible personality change.[102] He or she has a sense of foreshortened future without expectation of a career, marriage, children or normal lifespan.

(f) *Dissociation, depersonalization and atypical behaviour*

244. Dissociation is a disruption in the integration of consciousness, self-perception, memory and actions. A person may be cut off or unaware of certain actions or may feel split in two as if observing him or herself from a distance. Depersonalization is feeling detached from oneself or one's body. Impulse control problems result in behaviours that the survivor considers highly atypical with respect to his or her pre-trauma personality. A previously cautious individual may engage in high-risk behaviour.

(g) *Somatic complaints*

245. Somatic symptoms such as pain, headache or other physical complaints, with or without objective findings, are common problems among torture victims. Pain may be the only manifest complaint and may shift in location and vary in intensity. Somatic symptoms can be directly due to physical consequences of torture or psychological in origin. For example, pain of all kinds may be a direct physical consequence of torture or of psychological origin. Typical somatic complaints include back pain, musculoskeletal pain and headaches, often from head injuries. Headaches are very common among torture survivors and often lead to chronic post-traumatic headaches. They may also be caused or exacerbated by tension and stress.

(h) *Sexual dysfunction*

246. Sexual dysfunction is common among survivors of torture, particularly among those who have suffered sexual torture or rape, but not exclusively (see chapter V, sect. D.8).

(i) *Psychosis*

247. Cultural and linguistic differences may be confused with psychotic symptoms. Before labelling some-

one as psychotic, the symptoms must be evaluated within the individual's unique cultural context. Psychotic reactions may be brief or prolonged, and the symptoms may occur while the person is detained and tortured or afterwards. The following findings are possible:

    (i) Delusions;

    (ii) Auditory, visual, tactile and olfactory hallucinations;

    (iii) Bizarre ideation and behaviour;

    (iv) Illusions or perceptual distortions that may take the form of pseudo-hallucinations and border on true psychotic states. False perceptions and hallucinations that occur on falling asleep or on waking are common among the general population and do not denote psychosis. It is not uncommon for torture victims to report occasionally hearing screams, their name being called or seeing shadows, but not to have florid signs or symptoms of psychosis;

    (v) Paranoia and delusions of persecution;

    (vi) Recurrence of psychotic disorders or mood disorders with psychotic features may develop among those who have a past history of mental illness. Individuals with a past history of bipolar disorder, recurrent major depression with psychotic features, schizophrenia and schizoaffective disorder may experience an episode of that disorder.

(j) *Substance abuse*

248. Alcohol and drug abuse often develop secondarily in torture survivors as a way of obliterating traumatic memories, regulating affects and managing anxiety.

(k) *Neuropsychological impairment*

249. Torture can cause physical trauma that leads to various levels of brain impairment. Blows to the head, suffocation and prolonged malnutrition may have long-term neurological and neuropsychological consequences that may not be readily assessed during the course of a medical examination. As in all cases of brain impairment that cannot be documented through head imaging or other medical procedures, neuropsychological assessment and testing may be the only reliable way of documenting the effects. Frequently, the target symptoms for such assessments have significant overlap with the symptomatology arising from PTSD and major depressive disorder. Fluctuations or deficits in level of consciousness, orientation, attention, concentration, memory and executive functioning may result from functional disturbances as well as have organic causes. Therefore, specialized skill in neuropsychological assessment and awareness of problems in cross-cultural validation of neuropsychological instruments are necessary when such distinctions are to be made (see section C.4 below).

3. *Diagnostic classifications*

250. While the chief complaints and most prominent findings among torture survivors are widely diverse and relate to the individual's unique life experiences and his or

---

[102] N. R. Holtan, "How medical assessment of victims of torture relates to psychiatric care", *Caring for Victims of Torture*, J. M. Jaranson and M. K. Popkin, eds. (Washington, D. C., American Psychiatric Press, 1998), pp. 107-113.

her cultural, social and political context, it is wise for evaluators to become familiar with the most commonly diagnosed disorders among trauma and torture survivors. Also, it is not uncommon for more than one mental disorder to be present, as there is considerable co-morbidity among trauma-related mental disorders. Various manifestations of anxiety and depression are the most common symptoms resulting from torture. Not infrequently, the symptomatology described above will be classified within the categories of anxiety and mood disorders. The two prominent classification systems are the International Classification of Disease (ICD-10)[103] classification of mental and behavioural disorders and the American Psychiatric Association's *Diagnostic and Statistical Manual of Mental Disorders* (DSM-IV).[104] For complete descriptions of diagnostic categories, the reader should refer to ICD-10 and DSM-IV. This review will focus on the most common trauma-related diagnoses: PTSD, major depression and enduring personality changes.

(a) *Depressive disorders*

251. Depressive states are almost ubiquitous among survivors of torture. In the context of evaluating the consequences of torture, it is problematic to assume that PTSD and major depressive disorder are two separate disease entities with clearly distinguishable aetiologies. Depressive disorders include major depressive disorder, single episode or major depressive disorder and recurrent (more than one episode). Depressive disorders can be present with or without psychotic, catatonic, melancholic or atypical features. According to DSM-IV, in order to make a diagnosis of major depressive episode, five or more of the following symptoms must be present during the same two-week period and represent a change from previous functioning (at least one of the symptoms must be depressed mood or loss of interest or pleasure): (1) depressed mood; (2) markedly diminished interest or pleasure in all or almost all activities; (3) weight loss or change of appetite; (4) insomnia or hypersomnia; (5) psychomotor agitation or retardation; (6) fatigue or loss of energy; (7) feelings of worthlessness or excessive or inappropriate guilt; (8) diminished ability to think or concentrate; and (9) recurrent thoughts of death or suicide. To make this diagnosis the symptoms must cause significant distress or impaired social or occupational functioning, not be due to a physiological disorder and unaccounted for by another DSM-IV diagnosis.

(b) *Post-traumatic stress disorder*

252. The diagnosis most commonly associated with the psychological consequences of torture is PTSD. The association between torture and this diagnosis has become very strong in the minds of health providers, immigration courts and the informed lay public. This has created the mistaken and simplistic impression that PTSD is the main psychological consequence of torture.

253. The DSM-IV definition of PTSD relies heavily on the presence of memory disturbances in relation to the trauma, such as intrusive memories, nightmares and the inability to recall important aspects of the trauma. The individual may be unable to recall with precision specific details of the torture events but will be able to recall the major themes of the torture experiences. For example, the victim may be able to recall being raped on several occasions but not be able to give the exact dates, locations and details of the setting or the perpetrators. Under such circumstances, the inability to recall precise details supports, rather than discounts, the credibility of a survivor's story. Major themes in the story will be consistent upon re-interviewing. The ICD-10 diagnosis of PTSD is very similar to that of DSM-IV. According to DSM-IV, PTSD can be acute, chronic or delayed. The symptoms must be present for more than one month and the disturbance must cause significant distress or impairment in functioning. In order to diagnose PTSD, the individual must have been exposed to a traumatic event that involved life-threatening experiences for the victim or others and produced intense fear, helplessness or horror. The event must be re-experienced persistently in one or more of the following ways: intrusive distressing recollections of the event, recurrent distressing dreams of the event, acting or feeling as if the event were happening again including hallucinations, flashbacks and illusions, intense psychological distress at exposure to reminders of the event and physiological reactivity when exposed to cues that resemble or symbolize aspects of the event.

254. The individual must persistently demonstrate avoidance of stimuli associated with the traumatic event or show general numbing of responsiveness as indicated by at least three of the following: (1) efforts to avoid thoughts, feelings or conversations associated with the trauma; (2) efforts to avoid activities, places or people that remind the victim of the trauma; (3) inability to recall an important aspect of the event; (4) diminished interest in significant activities; (5) detachment or estrangement from others; (6) restricted affect; and (7) foreshortened sense of future. Another reason to make a DSM-IV diagnosis of PTSD is the persistence of symptoms of increased arousal that were not present before the trauma, as indicated by at least two of the following: difficulty falling or staying asleep, irritability or angry outbursts, difficulty concentrating, hypervigilance and exaggerated startle response.

255. Symptoms of PTSD can be chronic or fluctuate over extended periods of time. During some intervals, symptoms of hyperarousal and irritability dominate the clinical picture. At these times, the survivor will usually also report increased intrusive memories, nightmares and flashbacks. At other times, the survivor may appear relatively asymptomatic or emotionally constricted and withdrawn. It must be kept in mind that not meeting diagnostic criteria of PTSD does not mean that torture was not inflicted. According to ICD-10, in a certain proportion of cases PTSD may follow a chronic course over many years with eventual transition to an enduring personality change.

[103] World Health Organization, *The ICD-10 Classification of Mental and Behavioural Disorders* (Geneva, 1994).

[104] American Psychiatric Association, *Diagnostic and Statistical Manual of Mental Disorders*: DSM-IV-TR, 4th ed. (Washington, D.C., 1994).

(c) *Enduring personality change*

256. After catastrophic or prolonged extreme stress, disorders of adult personality may develop in persons with no previous personality disorder. The types of extreme stress that can change the personality include concentration camp experiences, disasters, prolonged captivity with an imminent possibility of being killed, exposure to life-threatening situations, such as being a victim of terrorism, and torture. According to ICD-10, the diagnosis of an enduring change in personality should be made only when there is evidence of a definite, significant and persistent change in the individual's pattern of perceiving, relating or thinking about the environment and him or herself, associated with inflexible and maladaptive behaviours not present before the traumatic experience. The diagnosis excludes changes that are a manifestation of another mental disorder or a residual symptom of any antecedent mental disorder, as well as personality and behavioural changes due to brain disease, dysfunction or damage.

257. To make the ICD-10 diagnosis of enduring personality change after catastrophic experience, the changes in personality must be present for at least two years following exposure to catastrophic stress. ICD-10 specifies that the stress must be so extreme that "it is not necessary to consider personal vulnerability in order to explain its profound effect on the personality". This personality change is characterized by a hostile or distrustful attitude towards the world, social withdrawal, feelings of emptiness or hopelessness, a chronic feeling of "being on edge", as if constantly threatened, and estrangement.

(d) *Substance abuse*

258. Clinicians have observed that alcohol and drug abuse often develop secondarily in torture survivors as a way of suppressing traumatic memories, regulating unpleasant affects and managing anxiety. Although co-morbidity of PTSD with other disorders is common, systematic research has seldom studied the abuse of substances by torture survivors. The literature on populations that suffer from PTSD may include torture survivors, such as refugees, prisoners of war and veterans of armed conflicts, and may provide some insight. Studies of these groups reveal that prevalence of substance abuse varies by ethnic or cultural group. Former prisoners of war with PTSD were at increased risk of substance abuse, and combat veterans have high rates of co-morbidity of PTSD and substance abuse.[105, 106, 107, 108, 109, 110, 111, 112] In summary, there is considerable evidence from other populations at risk of PTSD that substance abuse is a potential co-morbid diagnosis for torture survivors.

(e) *Other diagnoses*

259. As is evident from the catalogue of symptoms described in this section, there are other diagnoses to be considered in addition to PTSD, such as major depressive disorder and enduring personality change. The other possible diagnoses include but are not limited to:

(i) Generalized anxiety disorder features excessive anxiety and worry about a variety of different events or activities, motor tension and increased autonomic activity;

(ii) Panic disorder is manifested by recurrent and unexpected attacks of intense fear or discomfort, including symptoms such as sweating, choking, trembling, rapid heart rate, dizziness, nausea, chills or hot flushes;

(iii) Acute stress disorder has essentially the same symptoms as PTSD but is diagnosed within one month of exposure to the traumatic event;

(iv) Somatoform disorders featuring physical symptoms that cannot be accounted for by a medical condition;

(v) Bipolar disorder featuring manic or hypomanic episodes with elevated, expansive or irritable mood, grandiosity, decreased need for sleep, flight of ideas, psychomotor agitation and associated psychotic phenomena;

(vi) Disorders due to a general medical condition often in the form of brain impairment with resultant fluctuations or deficits in level of consciousness, orientation, attention, concentration, memory and executive functioning;

(vii) Phobias such as social phobia and agoraphobia.

C. The psychological/psychiatric evaluation

1. *Ethical and clinical considerations*

260. Psychological evaluations can provide critical evidence of abuse among torture victims for several reasons: torture often causes devastating psychological symptoms, torture methods are often designed to leave no physical lesions and physical methods of torture may result in physical findings that either resolve or lack specificity.

---

[105] P. J. Farias, "Emotional distress and its socio-political correlates in Salvadoran refugees: analysis of a clinical sample", *Culture, Medicine and Psychiatry*, vol. 15 (1991), pp. 167-192.

[106] A. Dadfar, "The Afghans: bearing the scars of a forgotten war", *Amidst Peril and Pain: The Mental Health and Well-being of the World's Refugees*, A. Marsella and others (Washington, D. C., American Psychological Association, 1994).

[107] G. W. Beebe, "Follow-up studies of World War II and Korean war prisoners: II. Morbidity, disability, and malajustments", *American Journal of Epidemiology*, vol. 101 (1975), pp. 400-422.

[108] B. E. Engdahl and others, "Comorbidity and course of psychiatric disorders in a community sample of former prisoners of war", *American Journal of Psychiatry*, vol. 155 (1998), pp. 1740-1745.

[109] T. M. Keane and J. Wolfe, "Comorbidity in post-traumatic stress disorder: an analysis of community and clinical studies", *Journal of Applied Social Psychology*, vol. 20 (21) (1990), pp. 1776-1788.

[110] R. A. Kulka and others, *Trauma and the Vietnam War Generation: Report of Findings from the National Vietnam Veterans Readjustment Study* (New York, Brunner/Mazel, 1990).

[111] B. K. Jordan and others, "Lifetime and current prevalence of specific psychiatric disorders among Vietnam veterans and controls", *Archives of General Psychiatry*, vol. 48, No. 3 (1991), pp. 207-215.

[112] A. Y. Shalev, A. Bleich and R. J. Ursano, "Posttraumatic stress disorder: somatic comorbidity and effort tolerance", *Psychosomatics*, vol. 31 (1990), pp.197-203.

261. Psychological evaluations provide useful evidence for medico-legal examinations, political asylum applications, establishing conditions under which false confessions may have been obtained, understanding regional practices of torture, identifying the therapeutic needs of victims and as testimony in human rights investigations. The overall goal of a psychological evaluation is to assess the degree of consistency between an individual's account of torture and the psychological findings observed during the course of the evaluation. To this end, the evaluation should provide a detailed description of the individual's history, a mental status examination, an assessment of social functioning and the formulation of clinical impressions (see chapters III, sect. C, and IV, sect. E). A psychiatric diagnosis should be made, if appropriate. Because psychological symptoms are so prevalent among survivors of torture, it is highly advisable for any evaluation of torture to include a psychological assessment.

262. The assessment of psychological status and the formulation of a clinical diagnosis should always be made with an awareness of the cultural context. Awareness of culture-specific syndromes and native language-bound idioms of distress through which symptoms are communicated is of paramount importance for conducting the interview and formulating the clinical impression and conclusion. When the interviewer has little or no knowledge of the victim's culture, the assistance of an interpreter is essential. Ideally, an interpreter from the victim's country knows the language, customs, religious traditions and other beliefs that must be taken into account during the investigation. The interview may induce fear and mistrust on the part of the victim and possibly remind him or her of previous interrogations. To reduce the effects of re-traumatization, the clinician should communicate a sense of understanding of the individual's experiences and cultural background. It is inappropriate to observe the strict "clinical neutrality" that is used in some forms of psychotherapy, during which the clinician is inactive and says little. The clinician should communicate that he or she is an ally of the individual and adopt a supportive, non-judgemental approach.

2. *The interview process*

263. The clinician should introduce the interview process in a manner that explains in detail the procedures to be followed (questions asked about psychosocial history, including history of torture and current psychological functioning) and that prepares the individual for the difficult emotional reactions that the questions may provoke. The individual needs to be given an opportunity to request breaks, interrupt the interview at any time and be able to leave if the stress becomes intolerable, with the option of a later appointment. Clinicians need to be sensitive and empathic in their questioning, while remaining objective in their clinical assessment. At the same time, the interviewer should be aware of potential personal reactions to the survivor and the descriptions of torture that might influence the interviewer's perceptions and judgements.

264. The interview process may remind the survivor of interrogation during torture. Therefore, strong negative feelings towards the clinician may develop, such as fear, rage, revulsion, helplessness, confusion, panic or hatred. The clinician should allow for the expression and explanation of such feelings and express understanding for the individual's difficult predicament. In addition, the possibility that the person may still be persecuted or oppressed has to be kept in mind. When necessary, questions about forbidden activities should be avoided. It is important to consider the reasons for the psychological evaluation, as they will determine the level of confidentiality to which the expert is bound. If an evaluation of the credibility of an individual's report of torture is requested within the framework of a judicial procedure by a State authority, the person to be evaluated must be told that this implies lifting medical confidentiality for all the information presented in the report. However, if the request for the psychological evaluation comes from the tortured person, the expert must respect medical confidentiality.

265. Clinicians who conduct physical or psychological evaluations should be aware of the potential emotional reactions that evaluations of severe trauma may elicit in the interviewee and interviewer. These emotional reactions are known as transference and countertransference. Mistrust, fear, shame, rage and guilt are among the typical reactions that torture survivors experience, particularly when being asked to recount or remember details of their trauma. Transference refers to the feelings a survivor has towards the clinician that relate to past experiences but which are misunderstood as directed towards the clinician personally. In addition, the clinician's emotional response to the torture survivor, known as countertransference, may affect the psychological evaluation. Transference and countertransference are mutually interdependent and interactive.

266. The potential impact of transference reactions on the evaluation process becomes evident when it is considered that an interview or examination that involves recounting and remembering the details of a traumatic history will result in exposure to distressing and unwanted memories, thoughts and feelings. Thus, even though a torture victim may consent to an evaluation with the hope of benefiting from it, the resulting exposure may renew the trauma experience itself. This may include the following phenomena.

267. The evaluator's questions may be experienced as forced exposure akin to an interrogation. The evaluator may be suspected of having voyeuristic or sadistic motivations, and the interviewee may ask him or herself questions such as: "Why does he or she make me reveal every last terrible detail of what happened to me? Why would a normal person choose to listen to stories like mine in order to make a living? The evaluator must have some strange kind of motivation." There may be prejudices towards the evaluator because he or she has not been arrested and tortured. This may lead the subject to perceive the evaluator as being on the side of the enemy.

268. The evaluator is perceived as a person in a position of authority, which is often the case, and for that reason may not be trusted with certain aspects of the trauma history. Alternatively, as is often the case with subjects still in custody, the subject may be too trusting in situations where the interviewer cannot guarantee that there

will be no reprisals. Every precaution should be taken to ensure that prisoners do not put themselves at risk unnecessarily, naively trusting the outsider to protect them. Torture victims may fear that information that is revealed in the context of an evaluation cannot be safely kept from persecuting governments. Fear and mistrust may be particularly strong in cases where physicians or other health workers have been participants in the torture.

269. In many circumstances, the evaluator will be a member of the majority culture and ethnicity, whereas the subject, in the situation of the interview, will belong to a minority group or culture. This dynamic of inequality may reinforce the perceived and real imbalance of power and may increase the potential sense of fear, mistrust and forced submission in the subject. In some cases, particularly with subjects still in custody, this dynamic may relate more to the interpreter than to the evaluator. Ideally, therefore, the interpreter should also be an outsider and not be recruited locally, so that he or she can be seen by all to be as independent as the investigator. Of course, a family member on whom the authorities can later apply pressure to find out what was discussed in the evaluation should not be used as an interpreter.

270. If the evaluator and the victim are of the same gender, the interview may be more readily perceived as directly resembling the torture situation than if the genders were different. For example, a woman who was raped or tortured in prison by a male guard is likely to experience more distress, mistrust and fear when facing a male evaluator than she might with a female interviewer. The opposite is true for men who have been assaulted sexually. They may be ashamed to tell the details of their torture to a female evaluator. Experience has shown, particularly in cases of victims still in custody, that in all but the most traditionally fundamentalist societies (where it is out of the question for a male to even interview, let alone examine, a woman), it may be much more important that the interviewer be a physician to whom the victim can ask precise questions, rather than not being a male as in a case of rape. Victims of rape have been known to say nothing to non-medical female investigators, but to request to talk to a physician, even if male, so as to be able to ask specific medical questions. Typical questions are about possible sequelae, such as being pregnant, being able to conceive later on or about the future of sexual relations between spouses. In the context of evaluations conducted for legal purposes, the necessary attention to detail and precise questioning about history are easily perceived as a sign of mistrust or doubt on the part of the examiner.

271. Because of the psychological pressures mentioned earlier, survivors may be re-traumatized and overwhelmed by memories and, as a result, affect or mobilize strong defences that result in profound withdrawal and affective flattening during examination or interview. For the purposes of documentation, the withdrawal and flattening present special difficulties because torture victims may be unable to communicate their history and current suffering effectively, although it would be most beneficial for them to do so.

272. Countertransference reactions are often unconscious, and when a person is unaware of countertransfer-ence, it becomes a problem. Having feelings when listening to individuals speak of their torture is to be expected, although these feelings can interfere with the clinician's effectiveness, but when understood they can guide the clinician. Physicians and psychologists involved in the evaluation and treatment of torture victims agree that awareness and understanding of typical countertransference reactions are crucial because countertransference can have significantly limiting effects on the ability to evaluate and document the physical and psychological consequences of torture. Effective documentation of torture and other forms of ill-treatment requires an understanding of personal motivations for working in this area. There is a consensus that professionals who continuously conduct this kind of examination should obtain supervision and professional support from peers who are experienced in this field. Common countertransference reactions include:

(a) Avoidance, withdrawal and defensive indifference in reaction to being exposed to disturbing material. This may lead to forgetting some details and underestimating the severity of physical or psychological consequences;

(b) Disillusionment, helplessness, hopelessness and overidentification that may lead to symptoms of depression or vicarious traumatization, such as nightmares, anxiety and fear;

(c) Omnipotence and grandiosity in the form of feeling like a saviour, the great expert on trauma or the last hope for the survivor's recovery and well-being;

(d) Feelings of insecurity about professional skills when faced with the gravity of the reported history or suffering. This may manifest as lack of confidence in the ability to do justice to the survivor and unrealistic preoccupation with idealized medical norms;

(e) Feelings of guilt over not sharing the torture survivor's experience and pain or over the awareness of what has not been done on a political level may result in overly sentimental or idealized approaches to the survivor;

(f) Anger and rage towards torturers and persecutors are expectable, but may undermine the ability to maintain objectivity when they are driven by unrecognized personal experiences and thus become chronic or excessive;

(g) Anger or repugnance against the victim may arise as a result of feeling exposed to unaccustomed levels of anxiety. This may also arise as a result of feeling used by the victim when the clinician experiences doubt about the truth of the alleged torture history and the victim stands to benefit from an evaluation that documents the consequences of the alleged incident;

(h) Significant differences between the cultural value systems of the clinician and the individual alleging torture may include belief in myths about ethnic groups, condescending attitudes and underestimation of the individual's sophistication or capacity for insight. Conversely, clinicians who are members of the same ethnic group as a victim might form a non-verbalized alliance that can also affect the objectivity of the evaluation.

273. Most clinicians agree that many countertransference reactions are not merely examples of distortion but are important sources of information about the psychological state of the torture victim. The clinician's effectiveness can be compromised when countertransference is acted upon rather than reflected upon. Clinicians engaged in the evaluation and treatment of torture victims are advised to examine countertransference and obtain supervision and consultation from a colleague, if possible.

274. Circumstances may require that interviews be conducted by a clinician from a cultural or linguistic group different from that of the survivor. In such cases, there are two possible approaches; each with advantages and disadvantages. The interviewer can use literal, word-for-word translations provided by an interpreter (see chapter IV, sect. I). Alternatively, the interviewer can use a bicultural approach to interviewing. This approach consists of using an interviewing team composed of the investigating clinician and an interpreter, who provides linguistic interpretation and facilitates an understanding of cultural meanings attached to events, experiences, symptoms and idioms. Because the clinician often does not recognize relevant cultural, religious and social factors, a skilled interpreter will be able to point out and explain these issues to the clinician. If the interviewer is relying strictly on literal, word-for-word interpretation, this type of in-depth interpretation of information will not be available. On the other hand, if interpreters are expected to point out relevant cultural, religious and social factors to the clinician, it is crucial that they do not attempt to influence in any way the tortured person's responses to the clinician's questions. When literal translation is not used, the clinician needs to be sure that the interviewee's responses, as communicated by the interpreter, represent exclusively what the person said without additions or deletions by the interpreter. Regardless of the approach, the interpreter's identity and ethnic, cultural and political affiliation are important considerations in the choice of an interpreter. The torture victim will have to trust the interpreter to understand what he or she is saying and to communicate it accurately to the investigating clinician. Under no circumstances should the interpreter be a law enforcement official or government employee. A family member should never be used as an interpreter, in order to respect privacy. The investigating team must choose an independent interpreter.

3. Components of the psychological/psychiatric evaluation

275. The introduction should contain mention of the referral source, a summary of collateral sources (such as medical, legal and psychiatric records) and a description of the methods of assessment used (interviews, symptom inventories, checklists and neuropsychological testing).

(a) *History of torture and ill-treatment*

276. Every effort should be made to document the full history of torture, persecution and other relevant traumatic experiences (see chapter IV, sect. E). This part of the evaluation is often exhausting for the person being evaluated. Therefore, it may be necessary to proceed in several sessions. The interview should start with a general summary of events before eliciting the details of the torture experiences. The interviewer needs to know the legal issues at hand because that will determine the nature and amount of information necessary to achieve documentation of the facts.

(b) *Current psychological complaints*

277. An assessment of current psychological functioning constitutes the core of the evaluation. As severely brutalized prisoners of war and rape victims show a lifetime prevalence of PTSD of between 80 and 90 per cent, specific questions about the three DSM-IV categories of PTSD (re-experiencing of the traumatic event, avoidance or numbing of responsiveness, including amnesia, and increased arousal) need to be asked.[113, 114] Affective, cognitive and behavioural symptoms should be described in detail, and the frequency, as well as examples, of nightmares, hallucinations and startle response should be stated. An absence of symptoms can be due to the episodic or often delayed nature of PTSD or to denial of symptoms because of shame.

(c) *Post-torture history*

278. This component of the psychological evaluation seeks information about current life circumstances. It is important to inquire about current sources of stress, such as separation or loss of loved ones, flight from the home country and life in exile. The interviewer should also inquire about the individual's ability to be productive, earn a living, care for his or her family and the availability of social supports.

(d) *Pre-torture history*

279. If relevant, describe the victim's childhood, adolescence, early adulthood, his or her family background, family illnesses and family composition. There should also be a description of the victim's educational and occupational history. Describe any history of past trauma, such as childhood abuse, war trauma or domestic violence, as well as the victim's cultural and religious background.

280. The description of pre-trauma history is important to assess mental health status and level of psychosocial functioning of the torture victim prior to the traumatic events. In this way, the interviewer can compare the current mental health status with that of the individual before torture. In evaluating background information, the interviewer should keep in mind that the duration and severity of responses to trauma are affected by multiple factors. These factors include, but are not limited to, the circumstances of the torture, the perception and interpretation of torture by the victim, the social context before, during and after torture, community and peer resources and values and attitudes about traumatic experiences, political and

[113] B. O. Rothbaum and others, "A prospective examination of post-traumatic stress disorder in rape victims", *Journal of Traumatic Stress*, vol. 5 (1992), pp. 455-475.

[114] P. B. Sutker and others, "Cognitive deficits and psychopathology among former prisoners of war and combat veterans of the Korean conflict", *American Journal of Psychiatry*, vol. 148 (1991), pp. 62-72.

cultural factors, severity and duration of the traumatic events, genetic and biological vulnerabilities, developmental phase and age of the victim, prior history of trauma and pre-existing personality. In many interview situations, because of time limitations and other problems, it may be difficult to obtain this information. It is important, nonetheless, to obtain enough data about the individual's previous mental health and psychosocial functioning to form an impression of the degree to which torture has contributed to psychological problems.

(e) *Medical history*

281. The medical history summarizes pre-trauma health conditions, current health conditions, body pain, somatic complaints, use of medication and its side effects, relevant sexual history, past surgical procedures and other medical data (see chapter V, sect. B).

(f) *Psychiatric history*

282. Inquiries should be made about a history of mental or psychological disturbances, the nature of problems and whether they received treatment or required psychiatric hospitalization. The inquiry should also cover prior therapeutic use of psychotropic medication.

(g) *Substance use and abuse history*

283. The clinician should inquire about substance use before and after the torture, changes in the pattern of use and whether substances are being used to cope with insomnia or psychological/psychiatric problems. These substances are not only alcohol, cannabis and opium but also regional substances of abuse such as betel nut and many others.

(h) *Mental status examination*

284. The mental status examination begins the moment the clinician meets the subject. The interviewer should make note of the person's appearance, such as signs of malnutrition, lack of cleanliness, changes in motor activity during the interview, use of language, presence of eye contact, ability to relate to the interviewer and the means the individual uses to establish communication. The following components should be covered, and all aspects of the mental status examination should be included in the report of the psychological evaluation; aspects such as general appearance, motor activity, speech, mood and affect, thought content, thought process, suicidal and homicidal ideation and a cognitive examination (orientation, long-term memory, intermediate recall and immediate recall).

(i) *Assessment of social function*

285. Trauma and torture can directly and indirectly affect a person's ability to function. Torture can also indirectly cause loss of functioning and disability, if the psychological consequences of the experience impair the individual's ability to care for himself or herself, earn a living, support a family and pursue an education. The clinician should assess the individual's current level of functioning by inquiring about daily activities, social role (as housewife, student, worker), social and recreational activ-

ities and perception of health status. The interviewer should ask the individual to assess his or her own health condition, to state the presence or absence of feelings of chronic fatigue and to report potential changes in overall functioning.

(j) *Psychological testing and the use of checklists and questionnaires*

286. Little published data exist on the use of psychological testing (projective and objective personality tests) in the assessment of torture survivors. Also, psychological tests of personality lack cross-cultural validity. These factors combine to limit severely the utility of psychological testing in the evaluation of torture victims. Neuropsychological testing may, however, be helpful in assessing cases of brain injury resulting from torture (see section C.4 below). An individual who has survived torture may have trouble expressing in words his or her experiences and symptoms. In some cases, it may be helpful to use trauma event and symptom checklists or questionnaires. If the interviewer believes it may be helpful to use these, there are numerous questionnaires available, although none are specific to torture victims.

(k) *Clinical impression*

287. In formulating a clinical impression for the purposes of reporting psychological evidence of torture, the following important questions should be asked:

(i) Are the psychological findings consistent with the alleged report of torture?

(ii) Are the psychological findings expected or typical reactions to extreme stress within the cultural and social context of the individual?

(iii) Given the fluctuating course of trauma-related mental disorders over time, what is the time frame in relation to the torture events? Where is the individual in the course of recovery?

(iv) What are the coexisting stressors impinging on the individual (e.g. ongoing persecution, forced migration, exile, loss of family and social role)? What impact do these issues have on the individual?

(v) Which physical conditions contribute to the clinical picture? Pay special attention to head injury sustained during torture or detention;

(vi) Does the clinical picture suggest a false allegation of torture?

288. Clinicians should comment on the consistency of psychological findings and the extent to which these findings correlate with the alleged abuse. The emotional state and expression of the person during the interview, his or her symptoms, the history of detention and torture and the personal history prior to torture should be described. Factors such as the onset of specific symptoms related to the trauma, the specificity of any particular psychological findings and patterns of psychological functioning should be noted. Additional factors should be considered, such as forced migration, resettlement, difficulty of acculturation, language problems, unemployment, loss of home, family and social status. The relation-

ship and consistency between events and symptoms should be evaluated and described. Physical conditions, such as head trauma or brain injury, may require further evaluation. Neurological or neuropsychological assessment may be recommended.

289. If the survivor has symptom levels consistent with a DSM-IV or ICD-10 psychiatric diagnosis, the diagnosis should be stated. More than one diagnosis may be applicable. Again, it must be stressed that even though a diagnosis of a trauma-related mental disorder supports the claim of torture, not meeting criteria for a psychiatric diagnosis does not mean the person was not tortured. A survivor of torture may not have the level of symptoms required to meet diagnostic criteria for a DSM-IV or ICD-10 diagnosis fully. In these cases, as with all others, the symptoms that the survivor has and the torture story that he or she claims to have experienced should be considered as a whole. The degree of consistency between the torture story and the symptoms that the individual reports should be evaluated and described in the report.

290. It is important to recognize that some people falsely allege torture for a range of reasons and that others may exaggerate a relatively minor experience for personal or political reasons. The investigator must always be aware of these possibilities and try to identify potential reasons for exaggeration or fabrication. The clinician should keep in mind, however, that such fabrication requires detailed knowledge about trauma-related symptoms that individuals rarely possess. Inconsistencies in testimony can occur for a number of valid reasons, such as memory impairment due to brain injury, confusion, dissociation, cultural differences in perception of time or fragmentation and repression of traumatic memories. Effective documentation of psychological evidence of torture requires clinicians to have a capacity to evaluate consistencies and inconsistencies in the report. If the interviewer suspects fabrication, additional interviews should be scheduled to clarify inconsistencies in the report. Family or friends may be able to corroborate details of the story. If the clinician conducts additional examinations and still suspects fabrication, the clinician should refer the individual to another clinician and ask for the colleague's opinion. The suspicion of fabrication should be documented with the opinion of two clinicians.

(l) *Recommendations*

291. The recommendations resulting from the psychological evaluation depend on the question posed at the time the evaluation was requested. The issues under consideration may concern legal and judicial matters, asylum, resettlement or a need for treatment. Recommendations can be for further assessment, such as neuropsychological testing, medical or psychiatric treatment, or a need for security or asylum.

4. *Neuropsychological assessment*

292. Clinical neuropsychology is an applied science concerned with the behavioural expression of brain dysfunction. Neuropsychological assessment, in particular, is concerned with the measurement and classification of behavioural disturbances associated with organic brain impairment. The discipline has long been recognized as useful in discriminating between neurological and psychological conditions and in guiding treatment and rehabilitation of patients suffering from the consequences of various levels of brain damage. Neuropsychological evaluations of torture survivors are performed infrequently and to date there are no neuropsychological studies of torture survivors available in the literature. The following remarks are, therefore, limited to a discussion of general principles to guide health providers in understanding the utility of, and indications for, neuropsychological assessment of subjects suspected of being tortured. Before discussing the issues of utility and indications, it is essential to recognize the limitations of neuropsychological assessment in this population.

(a) *Limitations of neuropsychological assessment*

293. There are a number of common factors complicating the assessment of torture survivors in general that are outlined elsewhere in this manual. These factors apply to neuropsychological assessment in the same way as to a medical or psychological examination. Neuropsychological assessments may be limited by a number of additional factors, including lack of research on torture survivors, reliance on population-based norms, cultural and linguistic differences and re-traumatization of those who have experienced torture.

294. As mentioned above, very few references exist in the literature concerning the neuropsychological assessment of torture victims. The pertinent body of literature concerns various types of head trauma and the neuropsychological assessment of PTSD in general. Therefore, the following discussion and subsequent interpretations of neuropsychological assessments are necessarily based on the application of general principles used with other subject populations.

295. Neuropsychological assessment as it has been developed and practised in Western countries relies heavily on an actuarial approach. This approach typically involves comparing the results of a battery of standardized tests to population-based norms. Although norm-referenced interpretations of neuropsychological assessments may be supplemented by a Lurian approach of qualitative analysis, particularly when the clinical situation demands it, a reliance on the actuarial approach predominates.[115, 116] Moreover, a reliance on test scores is greatest when brain impairment is mild to moderate in severity, rather than severe, or when neuropsychological deficits are thought to be secondary to a psychiatric disorder.

296. Cultural and linguistic differences may significantly limit the utility and applicability of neuropsychological assessment among suspected torture victims. Neuropsychological assessments are of questionable validity when standard translations of tests are unavailable and the clinical examiner is not fluent in the subject's

[115] A. R. Luria and L. V. Majovski, "Basic approaches used in American and Soviet clinical neuropsychology", *American Psychologist*, vol. 32 (11) (1977), pp. 959-968.

[116] R. J. Ivnik, "Overstatement of differences", *American Psychologist*, vol. 33 (8) (1978), pp. 766-767.

language. Unless standardized translations of tests are available and examiners are fluent in the subject's language, verbal tasks cannot be administered at all and cannot be interpreted in a meaningful way. This means that only non-verbal tests can be used, and this precludes comparison between verbal and non-verbal faculties. In addition, an analysis of the lateralization (or localization) of deficits is more difficult. This analysis is often useful, however, because of the brain's asymmetrical organization, with the left hemisphere typically being dominant for speech. If population-based norms are unavailable for the subject's cultural and linguistic group, neuropsychological assessment is also of questionable validity. An estimate of IQ is one of the central benchmarks that allow examiners to place neuropsychological test scores into proper perspective. Within the population of the United States, for example, these estimates are often derived from verbal subsets using the Wechsler scales, particularly the information subscale, because in the presence of organic brain impairment, acquired factual knowledge is less likely to suffer deterioration than other tasks and be more representative of past learning ability than other measures. Measurement may also be based on educational and work history and demographic data. Obviously, neither one of these two considerations applies to subjects for whom population-based norms have not been established. Therefore, only very coarse estimates concerning pre-trauma intellectual functioning can be made. As a result, neuropsychological impairment that is anything less than severe or moderate may be difficult to interpret.

297. Neuropsychological assessments may re-traumatize those who have experienced torture. Great care must be taken in order to minimize any potential re-traumatization of the subject in any form of diagnostic procedure (see chapter IV, sect. H). To cite only one obvious example specific to neuropsychological testing, it would be potentially very damaging to proceed with a standard administration of the Halstead-Reitan Battery, in particular the Tactual Performance Test (TPT), and routinely blindfold the subject. For most torture victims who have experienced blindfolding during detention and torture, and even for those who were not blindfolded, it would be very traumatic to introduce the experience of helplessness inherent in this procedure. In fact, any form of neuropsychological testing in itself may be problematic, regardless of the instrument used. Being observed, timed with a stopwatch and asked to give maximum effort on an unfamiliar task, in addition to being asked to perform, rather than having a dialogue, may prove to be too stressful or reminiscent of the torture experience.

(b) *Indications for neuropsychological assessment*

298. In evaluating behavioural deficits in suspected torture victims, there are two primary indications for neuropsychological assessment: brain injury and PTSD plus related diagnoses. While both sets of conditions overlap in some aspects, and will often coincide, it is only the former that is a typical and traditional application of clinical neuropsychology, whereas the latter is relatively new, not well researched and rather problematic.

299. Brain injury and resulting brain damage may result from various types of head trauma and metabolic disturbances inflicted during periods of persecution, detention and torture. This may include gunshot wounds, the effects of poisoning, malnutrition as a result of starvation or forced ingestion of harmful substances, the effects of hypoxia or anoxia resulting from asphyxiation or near drowning and, most commonly, from blows to the head suffered during beatings. Blows to the head are frequently inflicted during periods of detention and torture. For example, in one sample of torture survivors, blows to the head were the second most frequently cited form of bodily abuse (45 per cent) behind blows to the body (58 per cent).[117] The potential for brain damage is high among torture victims.

300. Closed head injuries resulting in mild to moderate levels of long-term impairment are perhaps the most commonly assessed cause of neuropsychological abnormality. While signs of injury may include scars on the head, brain lesions cannot usually be detected by diagnostic imaging of the brain. Mild to moderate levels of brain damage might be overlooked or underestimated by mental health professionals because symptoms of depression and PTSD are likely to figure prominently in the clinical picture, resulting in less attention being paid to the potential effect of head trauma. Commonly, the subjective complaints of survivors include difficulties with attention, concentration and short-term memory, which can be the result of either brain impairment or PTSD. Since these complaints are common in survivors suffering from PTSD, the question whether they are actually due to head injury may not even be asked.

301. The diagnostician must rely, in an initial phase of the examination, on reported history of head trauma and the course of symptomatology. As is usually the case with brain-injured subjects, information from third parties, particularly relatives, may prove helpful. It must be remembered that brain-injured subjects often have great difficulty articulating or even appreciating their limitations because they are, so to speak, "inside" the problem. In gathering first impressions regarding the difference between organic brain impairment and PTSD, an assessment concerning the chronicity of symptoms is a helpful starting point. If symptoms of poor attention, concentration and memory are observed to fluctuate over time and to co-vary with levels of anxiety and depression, this is more likely due to the phasic nature of PTSD. On the other hand, if impairment seems to appear chronic, lacks fluctuation and is confirmed by family members, the possibility of brain impairment should be entertained, even in the initial absence of a clear history of head trauma.

302. Once there is a suspicion of organic brain impairment, the first step for a mental health professional is to consider a referral to a physician for further neurological examination. Depending on initial findings, the physician may then consult a neurologist or order diagnostic tests. An extensive medical work-up, specific neurological consultation and neuropsychological evaluation

[117] H. C. Traue, G. Schwarz-Langer and N. F. Gurris, "Extremtraumatisierung durch Folter: Die psychotherapeutische Arbeit der Behandlungszentren für Folteropfer", *Verhaltenstherapie und Verhaltensmedizin*, vol. 18 (1) (1997), pp. 41-62.

are among the possibilities to be considered. The use of neuropsychological evaluation procedures is usually indicated if there is a lack of gross neurological disturbance, reported symptoms are predominantly cognitive in nature or a differential diagnosis between brain impairment and PTSD has to be made.

303. The selection of neuropsychological tests and procedures is subject to the limitations specified above and, therefore, cannot follow a standard battery format, but rather must be case-specific and sensitive to individual characteristics. The flexibility required in the selection of tests and procedures demands considerable experience, knowledge and caution on the part of the examiner. As has been pointed out above, the range of instruments to be used will often be limited to non-verbal tasks, and the psychometric characteristics of any standardized tests will most likely suffer when population-based norms do not apply to an individual subject. An absence of verbal measures represents a very serious limitation. Many areas of cognitive functioning are mediated through language, and systematic comparisons between various verbal and non-verbal measures are typically used in order to arrive at conclusions regarding the nature of deficits.

304. What complicates matters further is evidence that significant inter-group differences in performances of non-verbal tasks have been found between relatively closely related cultures. For example, research compared the performance of randomly selected, community-based samples of 118 English-speaking and 118 Spanish-speaking elders on a brief neuropsychological test battery.[118] The samples were randomly selected and demographically matched. Yet, while scores on verbal measures were similar, the Spanish-speaking subjects scored significantly lower on almost all non-verbal measures. These results suggest that caution is warranted when using non-verbal and verbal measures to assess non-English-speaking individuals, when tests are prepared for English-speaking subjects.

305. The choice of instruments and procedures in neuropsychological assessment of suspected torture victims must be left to the individual clinician, who will have to select them in accordance with the demands and possibilities of the situation. Neuropsychological tests cannot be used properly without extensive training and knowledge in brain-behaviour relations. Comprehensive lists of neuropsychological procedures and tests and their proper application can be found in standard references.[119]

(c) *Post-traumatic stress disorder*

306. The considerations offered above should make it clear that great caution is needed when attempting neuropsychological assessment of brain impairment in suspected torture victims. This must be even more strongly the case in attempting to document PTSD in suspected survivors through neuropsychological assessment. Even in the case of assessing PTSD subjects for whom population-based norms are available, there are considerable difficulties to consider. PTSD is a psychiatric disorder and traditionally has not been the focus of neuropsychological assessment. Furthermore, PTSD does not conform to the classical paradigm of an analysis of identifiable brain lesions that can be confirmed by medical techniques. With an increased emphasis on and understanding of the biological mechanisms involved in psychiatric disorders generally, neuropsychological paradigms have been invoked more frequently than in the past. However, as has been pointed out, "… comparatively little has been written to date on PTSD from a neuropsychological perspective".[120]

307. There is great variability among the samples used for the study of neuropsychological measures in post-traumatic stress. This may account for the variability of the cognitive problems reported from these studies. It was pointed out that "clinical observations suggest that PTSD symptoms show the most overlap with the neurocognitive domains of attention, memory and executive functioning". This is consistent with complaints heard frequently from survivors of torture. Subjects complain of difficulties in concentrating and feeling unable to retain information and engage in planned, goal-directed activity.

308. Neuropsychological assessment methods appear able to identify the presence of neurocognitive deficits in PTSD, even though the specificity of these deficits is more difficult to establish. Some studies have documented the presence of deficits in PTSD subjects when compared to normal controls but they have failed to discriminate these subjects from matched psychiatric controls.[121, 122] In other words, it is likely that neurocognitive deficits on test performances will be evident in cases of PTSD, but insufficient for diagnosing it. As in many other types of assessment, interpretation of test results must be integrated into a larger context of interview information and possibly personality testing. In that sense, specific neuropsychological assessment methods can make a contribution to the documentation of PTSD in the same manner that they do for other psychiatric disorders associated with known neurocognitive deficits.

309. Despite significant limitations, neuropsychological assessment may be useful in evaluating individ-uals suspected of having brain injury and in distinguishing brain injury from PTSD. Neuropsychological assessment may also be used to evaluate specific symptoms, such as problems with memory that occur in PTSD and related disorders.

[118] D. M. Jacobs and others, "Cross-cultural neuropsychological assessment: a comparison of randomly selected, demographically matched cohorts of English and Spanish-speaking older adults", *Journal of Clinical and Experimental Neuropsychology*, vol. 19 (No. 3) (1997), pp. 331-339.

[119] O. Spreen and E. Strauss, *A Compendium of Neuropsychological Tests*, 2nd ed. (New York, Oxford University Press, 1998).

[120] J. A. Knight, "Neuropsychological assessment in posttraumatic stress disorder", *Assessing Psychological Trauma and PTSD*, J. P. Wilson and T. M. Keane, eds. (New York, Guilford Press, 1997).

[121] J. E. Dalton, S. L. Pederson and J. J. Ryan, "Effects of post-traumatic stress disorder on neuropsychological test performance", *International Journal of Clinical Neuropsychology*, vol. 11 (3) (1989), pp. 121-124.

[122] T. Gil and others, "Cognitive functioning in post-traumatic stress disorder", *Journal of Traumatic Stress*, vol. 3, No. 1 (1990), pp. 29-45.

5. Children and torture

310.   Torture can impact a child directly or indirectly. The impact can be due to the child's having been tortured or detained, the torture of parents or close family members or witnessing torture and violence. When individuals in a child's environment are tortured, the torture will inevitably have an impact on the child, albeit indirect, because torture affects the entire family and community of torture victims. A complete discussion of the psychological impact of torture on children and complete guidelines for conducting an evaluation of a child who has been tortured is beyond the scope of this manual. Nevertheless, several important points can be summarized.

311.   First, when evaluating a child who is suspected of having undergone or witnessed torture, the clinician must make sure that the child receives support from caring individuals and that he or she feels secure during the evaluation. This may require a parent or trusted care provider to be present during the evaluation. Second, the clinician must keep in mind that children do not often express their thoughts and emotions regarding trauma verbally, but rather behaviourally.[123] The degree to which children are able to verbalize thought and affect depends on the child's age, developmental level and other factors, such as family dynamics, personality characteristics and cultural norms.

312.   If a child has been physically or sexually assaulted, it is important, if at all possible, for the child to be seen by an expert in child abuse. Genital examination of children, likely to be experienced as traumatic, should be performed by clinicians experienced in interpreting the findings. Sometimes it is appropriate to videotape the examination so that other experts can give opinions on the physical findings without the child having to be examined again. It may be inappropriate to perform a full genital or anal examination without a general anaesthetic. Furthermore, the examiner should be aware that the examination itself may be reminiscent of the assault and it is possible that the child may make a spontaneous outcry or psychologically decompensate during the examination.

(a)   Developmental considerations

313.   A child's reactions to torture depend on age, developmental stage and cognitive skills. The younger the child, the more his or her experience and understanding of the traumatic event will be influenced by the immediate reactions and attitudes of caregivers following the event.[124] For children under the age of three who have experienced or witnessed torture, the protective and reassuring role of their caregivers is crucial.[125] The reactions of very young children to traumatic experiences typically involve hyperarousal, such as restlessness, sleep disturbance, irritability, heightened startle reactions and avoidance. Children over three often tend to withdraw and refuse to speak directly about traumatic experiences. The ability for verbal expression increases during development. A marked increase occurs around the concrete operational stage (8-9 years old), when children develop the ability to provide a reliable chronology of events. During this stage, concrete operations and temporal and spatial capacities develop.[126] These new skills are still fragile, and it is not usually until the beginning of the formal operational stage (12 years old) that children are consistently able to construct a coherent narrative. Adolescence is a turbulent developmental period. The effects of torture can vary widely. Torture experiences may cause profound personality changes in adolescents resulting in antisocial behaviour.[127] Alternatively, the effects of torture on adolescents may be similar to those seen in younger children.

(b)   Clinical considerations

314.   Symptoms of PTSD may appear in children. The symptoms can be similar to those observed in adults, but the clinician must rely more heavily on observations of the child's behaviour than on verbal expression.[128, 129, 130, 131] For example, the child may demonstrate symptoms of re-experiencing as manifested by monotonous, repetitive play representing aspects of the traumatic event, visual memories of the events in and out of play, repeated questions or declarations about the traumatic event and nightmares. The child may develop bedwetting, loss of control of bowel movements, social withdrawal, restricted affect, attitude changes towards self and others and feelings that there is no future. He or she may experience hyperarousal and have night terrors, problems going to bed, sleep disturbance, heightened startle response, irritability and significant disturbances in attention and concentration. Fears and aggressive behaviour that were non-existent before the traumatic event may appear as aggressiveness towards peers, adults or animals, fear of the dark, fear of going to the toilet alone and phobias. The child may demonstrate sexual behaviour that is inappropriate for his or her age and somatic reactions. Anxiety symptoms, such as exaggerated fear of strangers, separation anxiety, panic, agitation, temper tantrums and uncontrolled crying may appear. The child may also develop eating problems.

(c)   Role of the family

315.   The family plays an important dynamic role in persisting symptomatology among children. In order to preserve cohesion in the family, dysfunctional behaviours

[123] C. Schlar, "Evaluation and documentation of psychological evidence of torture", unpublished paper, 1999.

[124] S. von Overbeck Ottino, "Familles victimes de violences collectives et en exil : quelle urgence, quel modèle de soins ? Le point de vue d'une pédopsychiatre", Revue française de psychiatrie et de psychologie médicale, vol. 14 (1998), pp. 35-39.

[125] V. Grappe, "La guerre en ex-Yougoslavie: un regard sur les enfants réfugiés", Psychiatrie humanitaire en ex-Yougoslavie et en Arménie. Face au traumatisme, M. R. Moro and S. Lebovici, eds. (Paris, Presses universitaires de France, 1995).

[126] J. Piaget, La naissance de l'intelligence chez l'enfant (Neuchâtel, Delachaux et Niestlé, 1977).

[127] See footnote 125.

[128] L. C. Terr, "Childhood traumas: an outline and overview", American Journal of Psychiatry, vol. 148 (1991), pp. 10-20.

[129] National Center for Infants, Toddlers and Families, Zero to Three (1994).

[130] F. Sironi, "On torture un enfant, ou les avatars de l'ethnocentrisme psychologique", Enfances, No. 4 (1995), pp. 205-215.

[131] L. Bailly, Les catastrophes et leurs conséquences psycho-traumatiques chez l'enfant (Paris, ESF, 1996).

and delegation of roles may occur. Family members, often children, can be assigned the role of patient and develop severe disorders. A child may be overly protected or important facts about the trauma may be hidden. Alternatively, the child can be parentified and expected to care for the parents. When the child is not the direct victim of torture but only indirectly affected, adults often tend to underestimate the impact on the child's psyche and development. When loved ones around a child have been persecuted, raped and tortured or the child has witnessed severe trauma or torture, he or she may develop dysfunctional beliefs such as that he or she is responsible for the bad events or that he or she has to bear the parent's burdens. This type of belief can lead to long-term problems with guilt, loyalty conflicts, personal development and maturing into an independent adult.

Principles on the Effective Investigation and Documentation of Torture and Other Cruel, Inhuman or Degrading Treatment or Punishment*

1.   The purposes of effective investigation and documentation of torture and other cruel, inhuman or degrading treatment or punishment (hereinafter "torture or other ill-treatment") include the following:

   (*a*)   Clarification of the facts and establishment and acknowledgement of individual and State responsibility for victims and their families;

   (*b*)   Identification of measures needed to prevent recurrence;

   (*c*)   Facilitation of prosecution and/or, as appropriate, disciplinary sanctions for those indicated by the investigation as being responsible and demonstration of the need for full reparation and redress from the State, including fair and adequate financial compensation and provision of the means for medical care and rehabilitation.

2.   States shall ensure that complaints and reports of torture or ill-treatment are promptly and effectively investigated. Even in the absence of an express complaint, an investigation shall be undertaken if there are other indications that torture or ill-treatment might have occurred. The investigators, who shall be independent of the suspected perpetrators and the agency they serve, shall be competent and impartial. They shall have access to, or be empowered to commission investigations by, impartial medical or other experts. The methods used to carry out such investigations shall meet the highest professional standards and the findings shall be made public.

3.   (*a*)   The investigative authority shall have the power and obligation to obtain all the information necessary to the inquiry.[a] The persons conducting the investigation shall have at their disposal all the necessary budgetary and technical resources for effective investigation. They shall also have the authority to oblige all those acting in an official capacity allegedly involved in torture or ill-treatment to appear and testify. The same shall apply to any witness. To this end, the investigative authority shall be entitled to issue summonses to witnesses, including any officials allegedly involved, and to demand the production of evidence.

   (*b*)   Alleged victims of torture or ill-treatment, witnesses, those conducting the investigation and their families shall be protected from violence, threats of violence or any other form of intimidation that may arise pursuant to the investigation. Those potentially implicated in torture or ill-treatment shall be removed from any position of control or power, whether direct or indirect, over complainants, witnesses and their families, as well as those conducting the investigation.

4.   Alleged victims of torture or ill-treatment and their legal representatives shall be informed of, and have access to, any hearing, as well as to all information relevant to the investigation, and shall be entitled to present other evidence.

5.   (*a*)   In cases in which the established investigative procedures are inadequate because of insufficient expertise or suspected bias, or because of the apparent existence of a pattern of abuse or for other substantial reasons, States shall ensure that investiga-

---

*The Commission on Human Rights, in its resolution 2000/43, and the General Assembly, in its resolution 55/89, drew the attention of Governments to the Principles and strongly encouraged Governments to reflect upon the Principles as a useful tool in efforts to combat torture.

[a] Under certain circumstances, professional ethics may require information to be kept confidential. These requirements should be respected.

tions are undertaken through an independent commission of inquiry or similar procedure. Members of such a commission shall be chosen for their recognized impartiality, competence and independence as individuals. In particular, they shall be independent of any suspected perpetrators and the institutions or agencies they may serve. The commission shall have the authority to obtain all information necessary to the inquiry and shall conduct the inquiry as provided for under these Principles.[b]

(*b*)   A written report, made within a reasonable time, shall include the scope of the inquiry, procedures and methods used to evaluate evidence as well as conclusions and recommendations based on findings of fact and on applicable law. Upon completion, the report shall be made public. It shall also describe in detail specific events that were found to have occurred and the evidence upon which such findings were based and list the names of witnesses who testified, with the exception of those whose identities have been withheld for their own protection. The State shall, within a reasonable period of time, reply to the report of the investigation and, as appropriate, indicate steps to be taken in response.

6.   (*a*)   Medical experts involved in the investigation of torture or ill-treatment shall behave at all times in conformity with the highest ethical standards and, in particular, shall obtain informed consent before any examination is undertaken. The examination must conform to established standards of medical practice. In particular, examinations shall be conducted in private under the control of the medical expert and outside the presence of security agents and other government officials.

(*b*)   The medical expert shall promptly prepare an accurate written report, which shall include at least the following:

(i)   Circumstances of the interview: name of the subject and name and affiliation of those present at the examination; exact time and date; location, nature and address of the institution (including, where appropriate, the room) where the examination is being conducted (e.g., detention centre, clinic or house); circumstances of the subject at the time of the examination (e.g., nature of any restraints on arrival or during the examination, presence of security forces during the examination, demeanour of those accompanying the prisoner or threatening statements to the examiner); and any other relevant factors;

(ii)   History: detailed record of the subject's story as given during the interview, including alleged methods of torture or ill-treatment, times when torture or ill-treatment is alleged to have occurred and all complaints of physical and psychological symptoms;

(iii)   Physical and psychological examination: record of all physical and psychological findings on clinical examination, including appropriate diagnostic tests and, where possible, colour photographs of all injuries;

(iv)   Opinion: interpretation as to the probable relationship of the physical and psychological findings to possible torture or ill-treatment. A recommendation for any necessary medical and psychological treatment and/or further examination shall be given;

(v)   Authorship: the report shall clearly identify those carrying out the examination and shall be signed.

(*c*)   The report shall be confidential and communicated to the subject or his or her nominated representative. The views of the subject and his or her representative about the examination process shall be solicited and recorded in the report. It shall also be provided in writing, where appropriate, to the authority responsible for investigating the allegation of torture or ill-treatment. It is the responsibility of the State to ensure that it is delivered securely to these persons. The report shall not be made available to any other person, except with the consent of the subject or on the authorization of a court empowered to enforce such a transfer.

---

[b] See footnote (*a*) above.

Diagnostic tests

Diagnostic tests are being developed and evaluated all the time. The following tests were considered to be of value at the time of writing of this manual. However, when additional supporting evidence is required, investigators should attempt to find up-to-date sources of information, for example by approaching one of the specialized centres for the documentation of torture (see chapter V, sect. E).

1. *Radiological imaging*

In the acute phase of injury, various imaging modalities may be quite useful in providing additional documentation of skeletal and soft tissue injury. Once the physical injuries of torture have healed, however, the residual sequelae are generally no longer detectable by the same imaging methods. This is often true even when the survivor continues to suffer significant pain or disability from his or her injuries. Reference has already been made to various radiological studies in the discussion of the examination of the patient or in the context of various forms of torture. The following is a summary of the application of these methods. However, the more sophisticated and expensive technology is not universally available or at least not to a person in custody.

Radiological and imaging diagnostic examinations include routine radiographs (X-rays), radioisotopic scintigraphy, computerized tomography (CT), nuclear magnetic resonance imaging (MRI) and ultrasonography (USG). Each has advantages and disadvantages. X-rays, scintigraphy and CT use ionizing radiation, which may be a concern in cases of pregnant women and children. MRI uses a magnetic field. Potential biologic effects on foetuses and children are theoretical, but thought to be minimal. Ultrasound uses sound waves, and no biologic risk is known.

X-rays are readily available. Excluding the skull, all injured areas should have routine radiographs as the initial examination. While routine radiographs will demonstrate facial fractures, CT is a superior examination as it demonstrates more fractures, fragment displacement and associated soft tissue injury and complications. When periosteal damage or minimal fractures are suspected, bone scintigraphy should be used in addition to X-rays. A percentage of X-rays will be negative even when there is an acute fracture or early osteomyelitis. It is possible for a fracture to heal, leaving no radiographic evidence of previous injury. This is especially true in children. Routine radiographs are not the ideal examination for evaluation of soft tissue.

Scintigraphy is an examination of high sensitivity, but low specificity. It is an inexpensive and effective examination used to screen the entire skeleton for disease processes such as osteomyelitis or trauma. Testicular torsion can also be evaluated, but ultrasound is better suited to this task. Scintigraphy is not a method to identify soft tissue trauma. Scintigraphy can detect an acute fracture within 24 hours, but it generally takes two to three days and may occasionally take a week or more, particularly in the case of the elderly. The scan generally returns to normal after two years. However, it may remain positive for years in cases of fractures and cured osteomyelitis. The use of bone scintigraphy to detect fractures at the epiphysis or metadiaphysis (ends of long bones) in children is very difficult because of the normal uptake of the radiopharmaceutical at the epiphysis. Scintigraphy is often able to detect rib fractures that are not apparent on routine X-ray films.

(a) *Application of bone scintigraphy to the diagnosis of falanga*

Bone scans can be performed either with delayed images at about three hours or as a three-phase examination. The three phases are the radionucleide angiogram (arterial phase), blood pool images (venous phase, which is soft tissue) and delayed phase (bone phase). Patients examined soon after *falanga* should have two bone scans performed at one-week intervals. A negative first delayed scan and positive second scan indicate exposure to *falanga* within days before the first scan. In acute cases, two negative bone scans at an interval of one week do not necessarily mean that *falanga* did not occur, but that the severity of the *falanga* applied was below the sensitivity level of the scintigraphy. Initially, if three-phase scanning is done, increased uptake in the radionucleide angiogram phase and the blood pool images and no increase uptake in the bone phase would indicate hyperaemia compatible with soft tissue injury. Trauma in the foot bones and soft tissue can also be detected with MRI.[a]

(b) *Ultrasound*

Ultrasound is inexpensive and without biological hazard. The quality of an examination depends on the skill of the operator. Where CT is not available, ultrasound is used to evaluate acute abdominal trauma. Tendonopathy can also be evaluated by ultrasound, and it is a method of choice for testicular abnormalities. Shoulder ultrasound is carried out in the acute and chronic periods following

---

[a] See chapter V, footnotes 76 and 83; also refer to standard radiology and nuclear medicine texts for further information.

suspension torture. In the acute period, oedema, fluid collection on and around the shoulder joint, lacerations and haematomas of the rotator cuffs can be observed by ultrasound. Re-examination with ultrasound and finding that the evidence in the acute period disappears over time strengthen the diagnosis. In such cases, MRI, scintigraphy and other radiological examinations should be carried out together, and their correlation should be examined. Even without positive results from other examinations, ultrasound findings alone are adequate to prove suspension torture.

(c) Computerized tomography

CT is excellent for imaging soft tissue and bone. However, MRI is better for soft tissue than bone. MRI may detect an occult fracture before it can be imaged by either routine radiographs or scintigraphy. Use of open scanners and sedation may alleviate anxiety and claustrophobia, which are prevalent among torture survivors. CT is also excellent for diagnosing and evaluating fractures, especially temporal and facial bones. Other advantages include alignment and displacement of fragments, especially spinal, pelvic, shoulder and acetabular fractures. It cannot identify bone bruising. CT with and without intravenous infusion of a contrast agent should be the initial examination for acute, sub-acute and chronic central nervous system (CNS) lesions. If the examination is negative, equivocal or does not explain the survivor's CNS complaints or symptoms, proceed to MRI. CT with bone windows and a pre- and post-contrast examination should be the initial examination for temporal bone fractures. Bone windows may demonstrate fractures and ossicular disruption. The pre-contrast examination may demonstrate fluid and cholesteatoma. Contrast is recommended because of the common vascular anomalies that occur in this area. For rhinorrhea, injection of a contrast agent into the spinal canal should follow a temporal bone. MRI may also demonstrate the tear responsible for leakage of the fluid. When rhinorrhea is suspected, a CT of the face with soft tissue and bone windows should be performed. Then a CT should be obtained after a contrast agent is injected into the spinal canal.

(d) Magnetic resonance imaging

MRI is more sensitive than CT in detecting CNS abnormalities. The time course of CNS haemorrhage is divided into immediate, hyperacute, acute, sub-acute and chronic phases and CNS haemorrhage has ranges that correlate with imaging characteristics of the haemorrhage. Thus, the imaging findings may allow estimation of the timing of head injuries and correlation to alleged incidents. CNS haemorrhage may completely resolve or produce sufficient haemosiderin deposits for the CT to be positive even years later. Haemorrhage in soft tissue, especially in muscle, usually resolves completely, leaving no trace, but, in rare cases, it can ossify. This is called heterotrophic bone formation or *Myositis ossificans* and is detectable with CT.

2. Biopsy of electric shock injury

Electric shock injuries may, but do not necessarily, exhibit microscopic changes that are highly diagnostic and specific for electric current trauma. Absence of these specific changes in a biopsy specimen does not mitigate against a diagnosis of electric shock torture, and judicial authorities must not be permitted to make such an assumption. Unfortunately, if a court requests a petitioner alleging electric shock torture to submit to a biopsy for confirmation of the allegations, refusal to consent to the procedure or a negative result is bound to have a prejudicial impact on the court. Furthermore, clinical experience with biopsy diagnosis of torture-related electrical injury is limited, and the diagnosis can usually be made with confidence from the history and physical examination alone.

This procedure is, therefore, one that should be done in a clinical research setting and not promoted as a diagnostic standard. In giving informed consent for biopsy, the person must be informed of the uncertainty of the results and permitted to weigh the potential benefit against the impact upon an already traumatized psyche.

(a) Rationale for biopsy

There has been extensive laboratory research measuring the effects of electric shocks on the skin of anaesthetized pigs.[b,c,d,e,f,g] This work has shown that there are histologic findings specific to electrical injury that can be established by microscopic examination of punch biopsies of the lesions. However, further discussion of this research, which may have significant clinical application, is beyond the scope of this publication. The reader is referred to the footnote references for additional information.

Few cases of electric shock torture of humans have been studied histologically.[h,i,j,k] Only in one case, where

---

[b] H. K. Thomsen and others, "Early epidermal changes in heat and electrically injured pigskin: a light microscopic study", *Forensic Science International*, vol. 17 (1981), pp. 133-143.

[c] Ibid., "The effect of direct current, sodium hydroxide and hydrochloric acid on pig epidermis: a light microscopic and electron microscopic study", *Acta Pathol. Microbiol. Immunol. Scand*, vol. 91 (1983), pp. 307-316.

[d] H. K. Thomsen, "Electrically induced epidermal changes: a morphological study of porcine skin after transfer of low-moderate amounts of electrical energy", dissertation (University of Copenhagen, F.A.D.L., 1984), pp. 1-78.

[e] T. Karlsmark and others, "Tracing the use of torture: electrically induced calcification of collagen in pigskin", *Nature*, vol. 301 (1983), pp. 75-78.

[f] Ibid., "Electrically induced collagen calcification in pigskin: a histopathologic and histochemical study", *Forensic Science International*, vol. 39 (1988), pp. 163-174.

[g] T. Karlsmark, "Electrically induced dermal changes: a morphological study of porcine skin after transfer of low to moderate amounts of electrical energy", dissertation, University of Copenhagen, *Danish Medical Bulletin*, vol. 37 (1990), pp. 507-520.

[h] L. Danielsen and others, "Diagnosis of electrical skin injuries: a review and a description of a case", *American Journal of Forensic Medical Pathology*, vol.12 (1991), pp. 222-226.

[i] F. Öztop and others, "Signs of electrical torture on the skin", *Treatment and Rehabilitation Center Report 1994* (Human Rights Foundation of Turkey), vol. 11 (1994), pp. 97-104.

[j] L. Danielsen, T. Karlsmark, H. K. Thomsen, "Diagnosis of skin lesions following electrical torture", *Rom. J. Leg. Med.*, vol. 5 (1997), pp. 15-20.

[k] H. Jacobsen, "Electrically induced deposition of metal on the human skin", *Forensic Science International*, vol. 90 (1997), pp. 85-92.

lesions were probably excised seven days after the injury, were alterations in the skin believed to be diagnostic of the electrical injuries observed (deposition of calcium salts on dermal fibres in viable tissue located around necrotic tissue). Lesions excised a few days after alleged electrical torture in other cases have shown segmental changes and deposits of calcium salts on cellular structures highly consistent with the influence of an electrical current, but they are not diagnostic since deposits of calcium salts on dermal fibres were not observed. A biopsy taken one month after alleged electrical torture showed a conical scar, 1-2 millimetres wide, with an increased number of fibroblasts and tightly packed, thin collagen fibres, arranged parallel to the surface, consistent with but not diagnostic of electrical injury.

(b) *Method*

After receiving informed consent from the patient, and before biopsy, the lesion must be photographed using accepted forensic methods. Under local anaesthesia, a 3-4 millimetre punch biopsy is obtained, and placed in buffered formalin or a similar fixative. Skin biopsy should be performed as soon as possible after injury. Since electrical trauma is usually confined to the epidermis and superficial dermis, the lesions may quickly disappear. Biopsies can be taken from more than one lesion, but the potential distress to the patient must be taken into account.[l] Biopsy material should be examined by a pathologist experienced in dermatopathology.

(c) *Diagnostic findings for electrical injury*

Diagnostic findings for electrical injury include vesicular nuclei in epidermis, sweat glands and vessel walls (only one differential diagnosis: injuries via basic solutions) and deposits of calcium salts distinctly located on collagen and elastic fibres (the differential diagnosis, *Calcinosis cutis*, is a rare disorder only found in 75 of 220,000 consecutive human skin biopsies, and the calcium deposits are usually massive without distinct location on collagen and elastic fibres).[m]

Typical, but not diagnostic, findings for electrical injury are lesions appearing in conical segments, often 1-2 millimetres wide, deposits of iron or copper on epidermis (from the electrode) and homogenous cytoplasm in epidermis, sweat glands and vessel walls. There may also be deposits of calcium salts on cellular structures in segmental lesions or no abnormal histologic observations.

---

[l] S. Gürpinar and S. Korur Fincanci, "Insan Haklari Ihlalleri *ve* Hekim Sorumluluǧu" (Human rights violations and responsibility of the physician), *Birinci Basamak İçin Adli Tip El Kitabi* (Handbook of Forensic Medicine for General Practitioners) (Ankara, Turkish Medical Association, 1999).

[m] See footnote (h) above.

ANNEX III

Anatomical drawings for documentation of torture and ill-treatment

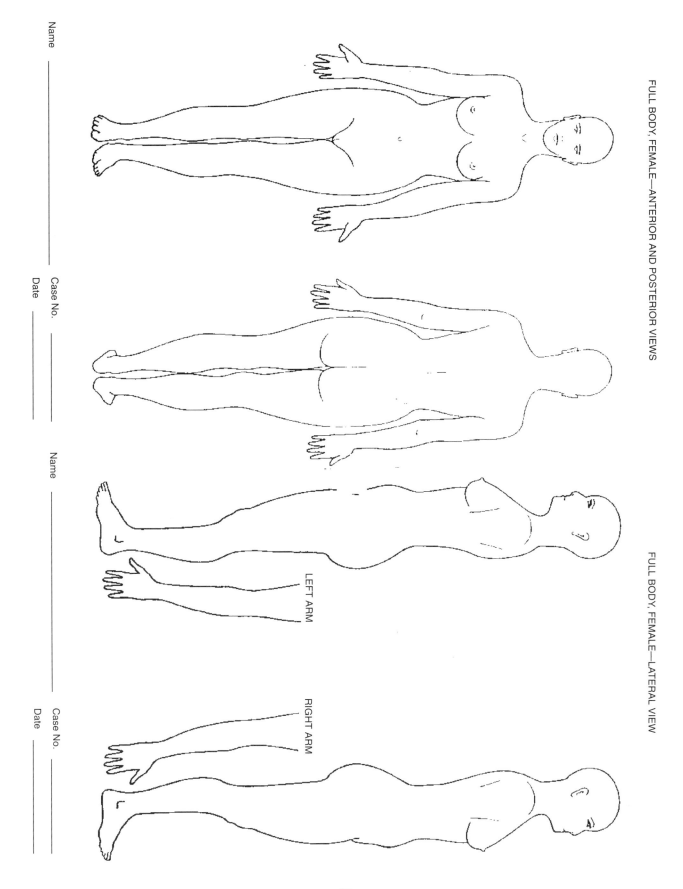

65

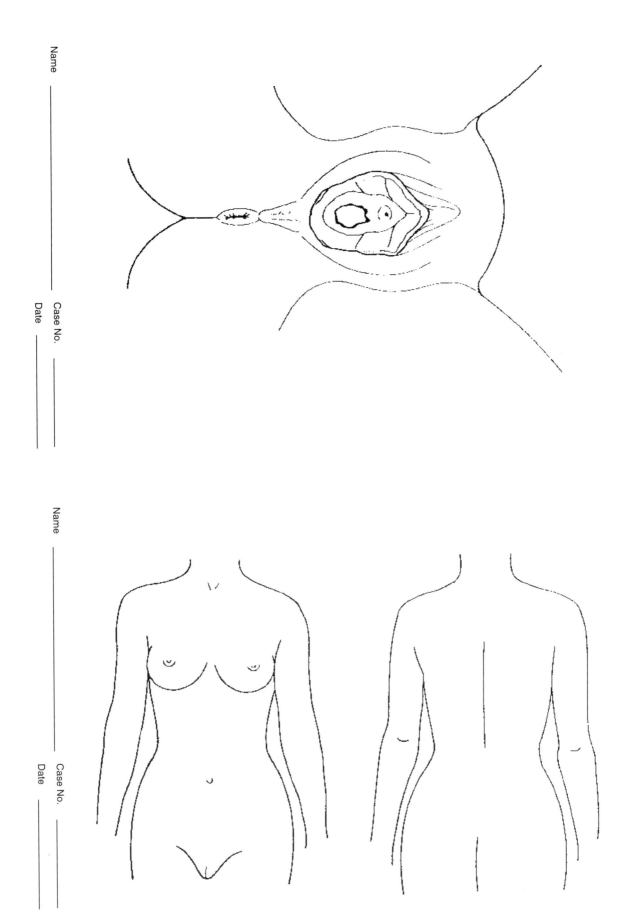

Name _____

Case No. _____

Date _____

Name _____

Case No. _____

Date _____

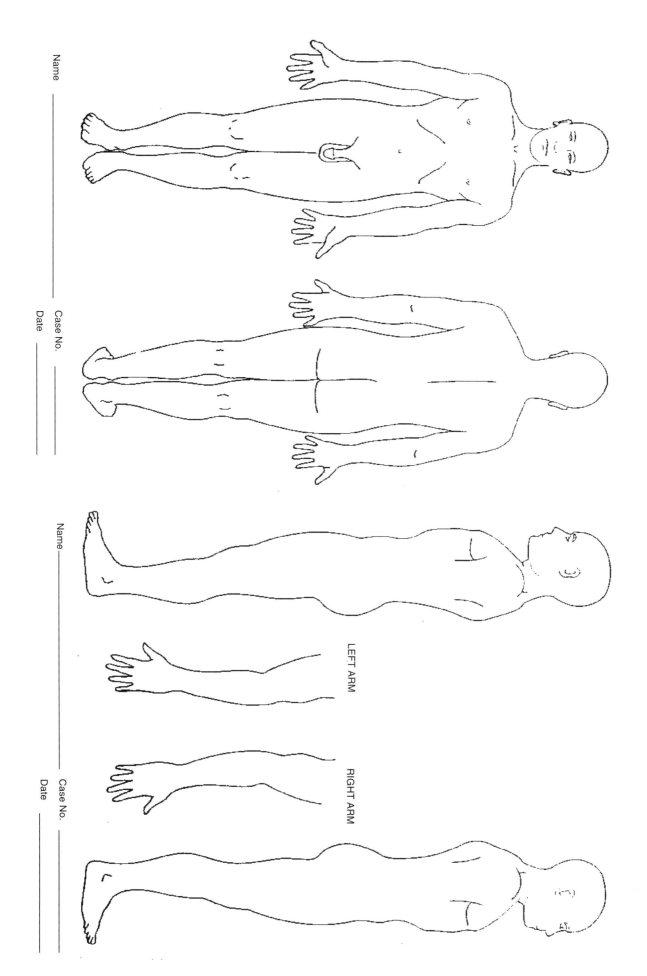

FULL BODY, MALE—ANTERIOR AND POSTERIOR VIEWS (VENTRAL AND DORSAL)

FULL BODY, MALE—LATERAL VIEW

LEFT ARM

RIGHT ARM

Name

Case No.

Date

Name

Case No.

Date

67

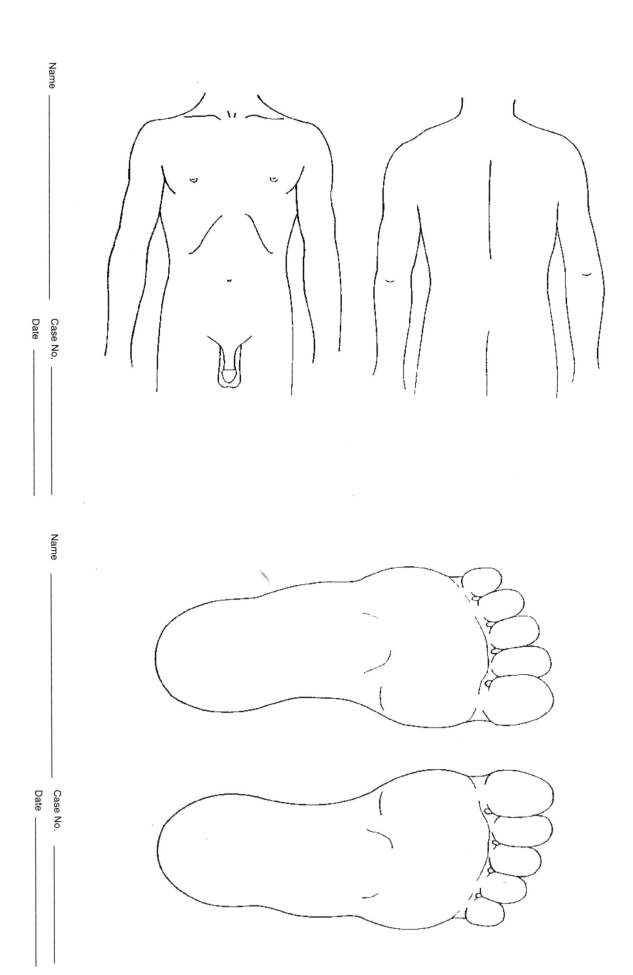

THORACIC ABDOMINAL, MALE—ANTERIOR AND POSTERIOR VIEWS

Name _____

Case No. _____

Date _____

FEET—LEFT AND RIGHT PLANTAR SURFACES

Name _____

Case No. _____

Date _____

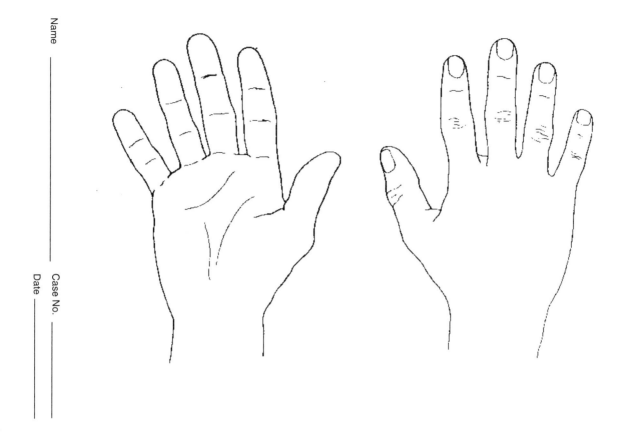
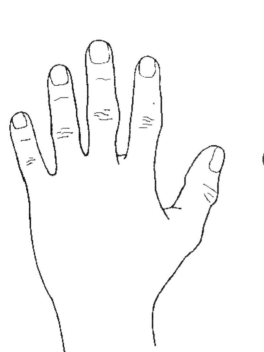
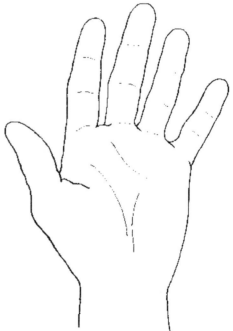

Name _____

Case No. _____

Date _____

Name _____

Case No. _____

Date _____

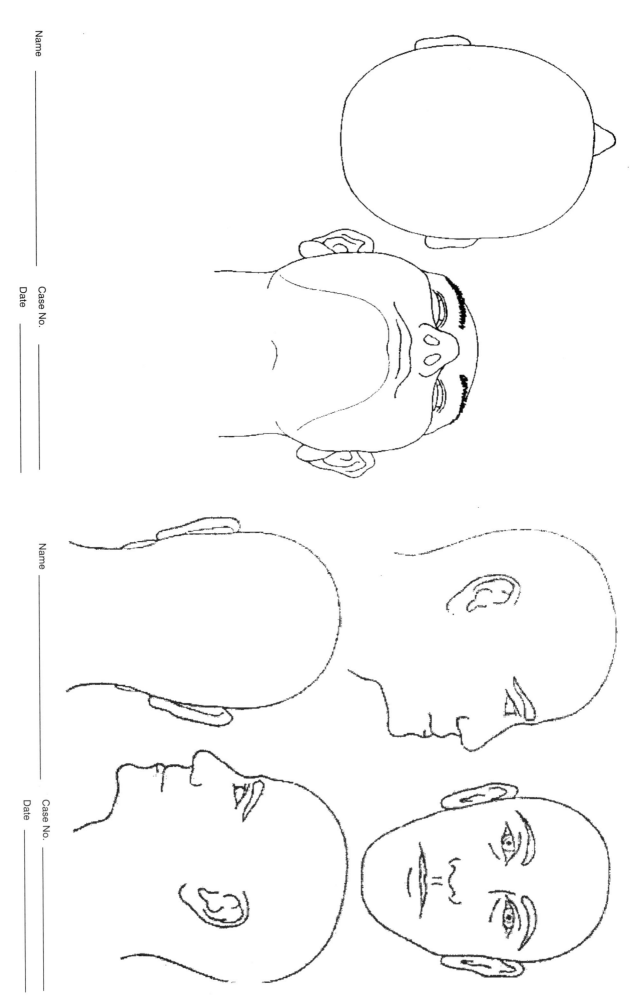

Name

Case No.

Date

Name

Case No.

Date

70

71

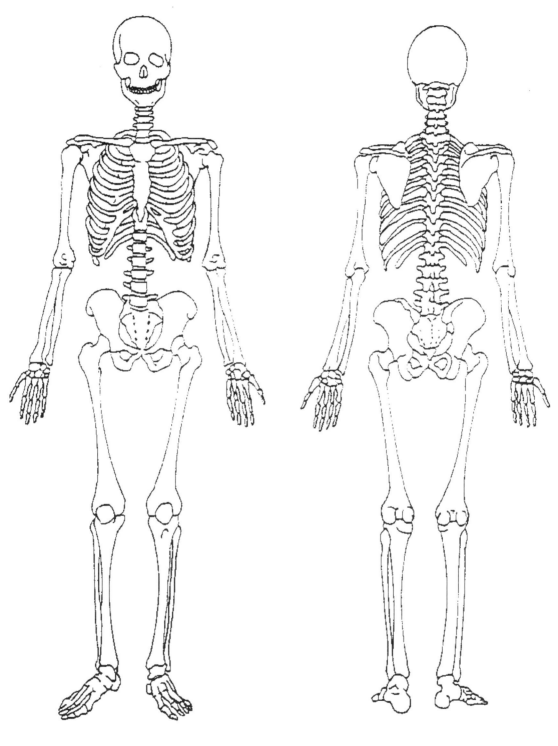

Name _____ Case No. _____

Date _____

MARK ALL EXISTING RESTORATIONS AND MISSING TEETH ON THIS CHART

Estimated   Age _____

Sex _____

Race _____

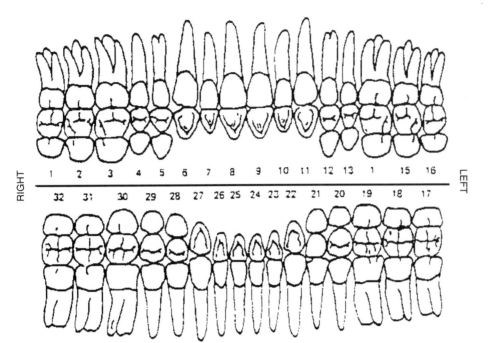

RIGHT

| 1 | 2 | 3 | 4 | 5 | 6 | 7 | 8 | 9 | 10 | 11 | 12 | 13 | 1 | 15 | 16 |

LEFT

| 32 | 31 | 30 | 29 | 28 | 27 | 25 | 24 | 23 | 22 | 21 | 20 | 19 | 18 | 17 |

Circle descriptive term

Prosthetic appliances present
Maxilla

Full denture

Partial denture

Fixed bridge

Mandible

Full denture

Partial denture

Fixed bridge

Describe completely all prosthetic appliances or fixed bridges

_____

_____

_____

_____

_____

Stains on teeth

Slight

Moderate

Severe

MARK ALL CARIES ON THIS CHART

Outline all caries and "X" out all missing teeth

Circle descriptive term

Relationship

Normal

Undershot

Overbite

RIGHT

| 1 | 2 | 3 | 4 | 5 | 6 | 7 | 8 | 9 | 10 | 11 | 12 | 13 | 14 | 15 | 16 |

LEFT

| 32 | 31 | 30 | 29 | 28 | 27 | 26 | 25 | 24 | 23 | 22 | 21 | 20 | 19 | 18 | 17 |

Periodontal Condition

Excellent

Average

Poor

Calculus

Slight

Moderate

Severe

Guidelines for the medical evaluation of torture and ill-treatment

The following guidelines are based on the *Istanbul Protocol: Manual on the Effective Investigation and Documentation of Torture and Other Cruel, Inhuman or Degrading Treatment or Punishment*. These guidelines are not intended to be a fixed prescription, but should be applied taking into account the purpose of the evaluation and after an assessment of available resources. Evaluation of physical and psychological evidence of torture and ill-treatment may be conducted by one or more clinicians, depending on their qualifications.

I. Case information

Date of exam: . . . .   Exam requested by (name/position): . . . .

Case or report No.: . . . . Duration of evaluation: . . . . . . hours . . . . minutes

Subject's given name: . . . . Birth date: . . . . Birth place: . . . .

Subject's family name: . . . . Gender: male/female: . . . .

Reason for exam: . . . . Subject's ID No.: . . . .

Clinician's name: . . . . Interpreter (yes/no), name: . . . .

Informed consent: yes/no   If no informed consent, why?: . . . .

Subject accompanied by (name/position): . . . .

Persons present during exam (name/position): . . . .

Subject restrained during exam: yes/no;   If "yes", how/why? . . . .

Medical report transferred to (name/position/ID No.): . . . .

   Transfer date: . . . . Transfer time: . . . .

Medical evaluation/investigation conducted without restriction (for subjects in custody): yes/no

   Provide details of any restrictions: . . . .

II. Clinician's qualifications (for judicial testimony)

Medical education and clinical training

Psychological/psychiatric training

Experience in documenting evidence of torture and ill-treatment

Regional human rights expertise relevant to the investigation

Relevant publications, presentations and training courses

Curriculum vitae.

III. Statement regarding veracity of testimony (for judicial testimony)

For example: "I personally know the facts stated below, except those stated on information and belief, which I believe to be true. I would be prepared to testify to the above statements based on my personal knowledge and belief."

IV. Background information

General information (age, occupation, education, family composition, etc.)

Past medical history

Review of prior medical evaluations of torture and ill-treatment

Psychosocial history pre-arrest.

V. Allegations of torture and ill-treatment

1. Summary of detention and abuse
2. Circumstances of arrest and detention
3. Initial and subsequent places of detention (chronology, transportation and detention conditions)
4. Narrative account of ill-treatment or torture (in each place of detention)
5. Review of torture methods.

VI. Physical symptoms and disabilities

Describe the development of acute and chronic symptoms and disabilities and the subsequent healing processes.

1. Acute symptoms and disabilities
2. Chronic symptoms and disabilities.

VII. Physical examination

1. General appearance
2. Skin
3. Face and head
4. Eyes, ears, nose and throat
5. Oral cavity and teeth
6. Chest and abdomen (including vital signs)
7. Genito-urinary system
8. Musculoskeletal system
9. Central and peripheral nervous system.

VIII. Psychological history/examination

1. Methods of assessment
2. Current psychological complaints
3. Post-torture history
4. Pre-torture history
5. Past psychological/psychiatric history
6. Substance use and abuse history
7. Mental status examination
8. Assessment of social functioning
9. Psychological testing: (see chapter VI, sect. C.1, for indications and limitations)
10. Neuropsychological testing (see chapter VI, sect. C.4, for indications and limitations).

IX.   Photographs

X.   Diagnostic test results (see annex II for indications and limitations)

XI.   Consultations

XII.   Interpretation of findings

1. Physical evidence

    A. Correlate the degree of consistency between the history of acute and chronic physical symptoms and disabilities with allegations of abuse.

    B. Correlate the degree of consistency between physical examination findings and allegations of abuse. (Note: The absence of physical findings does not exclude the possibility that torture or ill-treatment was inflicted.)

    C. Correlate the degree of consistency between examination findings of the individual with knowledge of torture methods and their common after-effects used in a particular region.

2. Psychological evidence

    A. Correlate the degree of consistency between the psychological findings and the report of alleged torture.

    B. Provide an assessment of whether the psychological findings are expected or typical reactions to extreme stress within the cultural and social context of the individual.

    C. Indicate the status of the individual in the fluctuating course of trauma-related mental disorders over time, i.e. what is the time frame in relation to the torture events and where in the course of recovery is the individual?

    D. Identify any coexisting stressors impinging on the individual (e.g. ongoing persecution, forced migration, exile, loss of family and social role, etc.) and the impact these may have on the individual.

    E. Mention physical conditions that may contribute to the clinical picture, especially with regard to possible evidence of head injury sustained during torture or detention.

XIII.   Conclusions and recommendations

1. Statement of opinion on the consistency between all sources of evidence cited above (physical and psychological findings, historical information, photographic findings, diagnostic test results, knowledge of regional practices of torture, consultation reports, etc.) and allegations of torture and ill-treatment.

2. Reiterate the symptoms and disabilities from which the individual continues to suffer as a result of the alleged abuse.

3. Provide any recommendations for further evaluation and care for the individual.

XIV.   Statement of truthfulness (for judicial testimony)

For example: "I declare under penalty of perjury, pursuant to the laws of .... (country), that the foregoing is true and correct and that this affidavit was executed on .... (date) at .... (city), ... (State or province)."

XV.   Statement of restrictions on the medical evaluation/investigation (for subjects in custody)

For example: "The undersigned clinicians personally certify that they were allowed to work freely and independently and permitted to speak with and examine (the subject) in private, without any restriction or reservation, and without any form of coercion being used by the detaining authorities"; or "The undersigned clinician(s) had to carry out his/her/their evaluation with the following restrictions: ...."

XVI.   Clinician's signature, date, place

XVII.   Relevant annexes

A copy of the clinician's curriculum vitae, anatomical drawings for identification of torture and ill-treatment, photographs, consultations and diagnostic test results, among others.

Further information can be obtained from: The Office of the United Nations High Commissioner for Human Rights, Palais des Nations, 1211 Geneva 10, Switzerland

Tel: (+41-22) 917 91 59
E-mail: infodesk@ohchr.org   *Internet*: www.ohchr.org